The Changing Corporate Image

Harold H. Marquis

American Management Association, Inc.

International standard book number: 0–8144–5236–1
Library of Congress catalog card number: 72–122584

FIRST PRINTING

Preface

CHANGE is accelerating in every aspect of business and industry, philosophical as well as technological, and there is no function of corporate management changing more rapidly than public attitudes and reactions. When consumer protests can wring from one of the largest and most successful corporations a series of explanations and apologies for the faults it stands accused of, the critical importance of the corporate image becomes apparent. When the president of another giant business states that the modern corporation may well be the most potent liberalizing force in our society, he reflects a growing attitude of management that was unheard of a generation ago.

It is no longer enough for a corporation to grow and pay taxes, to pay fair wages to its employees, to make good products and market them honestly. Every business faces new economic and social responsibilities. Many will be under pressure to meet new standards of employment equality, conservation of resources, reduction of pollution, safety of products, and effective warranties.

To live and grow, to command respect and regard, the corporate image must be more than a product of public relations. It must be an accurate and effective reflection of management's principles and practices, an accurate picture of what the company is and what it does. This image must be presented in terms stated by the public, not by business alone. To gain the support of customers, stockholders, employees, suppliers, competitors, government agencies, and the public, the corporate image must show that management is progressive, mobile, open to innovation, fair to all, and free of dogma and convention.

This book considers the problems management has in presenting a favorable image, and the opportunities and methods by which the image can be improved. It is based substantially on changes that have been made and are now being made, with specific examples and case histories. Consideration of these management functions will also be of interest to public relations and communications departments and to the agencies and counselors who work with management.

An analysis is made of the means by which an accurate evaluation of the existing image may be obtained, through both internal self-examination and outside research. From this base both long- and short-range objectives can be established. How to achieve these objectives is a major purpose of this book.

Harold H. Marquis

Contents

Three Case Histories

1

Image and Identity

THE corporate image, which is not only one of the important assets of a business but also a function of management, is receiving new attention and being modified in many companies around the world. These changes reflect economic and social changes and new corporate forms and activities, around which business and industry must plan for the future.

About 10 percent of all firms listed on the New York Stock Exchange have made substantial changes in their corporate images within the past decade. Of the 500 largest corporations listed by *Fortune*, nearly one-half have new names, new symbols, or new images. The 1968 edition of *Moody's Industrial Manual* reports more than 3,000 companies as *formerly* listed—they had either merged with other corporations or changed their names. Whichever action they took required a major change in a corporate image. The total merger picture quickened again in 1969, according to W. T. Grimm & Co., a Chicago consulting firm. The total was 6,132 corporate mergers for the year, up 37 percent from 1968.

Image and Identity Defined

The corporate image is the sum of all impressions of the firm in the public consciousness. It is an intangible impression that is different for each observer. The opinions of employees, customers, suppliers, stockholders, bankers, potential investors, competitors, government officials, and the general public all combine to form a *corporate image*. This is the feeling that the company creates with its products, business dealings, relations with communities, investments in the firm's securities, the appearance of its properties, and the way its personnel answers the telephone.

Corporate identity is that part of the image that can be seen or heard. It is every tangible mark of identity—all the vehicles, objects, and means of communication on which the corporate identity is displayed.

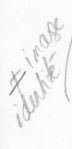

It is essential that this distinction between image and identity be understood. A new symbol or trademark often is an important part of an image-making program, but it by no means constitutes an image. An image exists in the minds of people, not only on the signs or letterheads of the corporation. Until the new image is communicated through every possible medium, there will not be a complete program.

In an earlier era, the products and services of a corporation would have been considered the principal components of its image. But this is a new era. Changes in products and innovations in business now come so fast that the products no longer carry the principal impact of the corporation. It is the overall management of the company, its continuing improvement of product lines and service, and its response to changing economic and social conditions that create a response in people's minds.

This change is further complicated by the increasing size of business enterprises and the advancing technology that tend to separate the company from human contacts. What management does on a broad scope and how these accomplishments are presented to various publics form the basis of its reputation and acceptance.

Kenneth Kramer, executive director of *Business Week,* expressed this point in a 1965 management seminar presented by the University of California and Walter Landor & Associates at the Visual Communications Center, San Francisco:

> It has been said quite rightly that we live today in a corporate society. However, the image of the corporation as a kindly parent, a great benefactor, a community "good citizen," a giant educator, manager of nat-

ural resources, a research pioneer, a principal generator of our economic growth is a fuzzy image indeed. Yet all these things are true. More believable is the contribution of a corporation in a material way—as a maker, seller, and supplier of goods.

The good deeds of corporations are hard to see but not difficult to find. Let me cite you one current example—the area of civil rights. Racial discrimination has been virtually eliminated in hotels, theaters, restaurants, offices, department stores, and factories. Accommodation to the new social code has been much slower in our schools, churches, labor unions, and voting.

Although the corporate image does not appear as such on the balance sheet, the goodwill represented by this image is one of the important assets of any corporation. Without the goodwill of customers, employees, suppliers, and financial sources, no company can long be successful.

The extent to which a firm gains the support of these important groups and of the general public depends on what it does to merit regard. The reflections of its achievements, the many ways in which a company is presented, form the image. There is as much skill involved in gaining a favorable image as in other phases of management.

Total Management Planning

Long-range plans for the corporate image should be an integral and important part of total management planning. How the company will appear in 2, 20, or 50 years will depend on what the company plans today. If the image is to be interpreted by public relations or communications department personnel, these men and women must be closely associated with basic planning. They must know the directions in which management plans to move the corporation before, not after, the moves are made.

In considering these plans, management should take into account the changes that can take place in the company, its industry, and its markets in every part of the world and in outer space.

A corporation must adjust to these changes in its policies as well as in its products or services. It will not be possible to set objectives that are based on present conditions and feel certain they can be accomplished. An ironclad policy and inflexible corporate image can easily become obsolete after the inevitable swift changes take place.

If there is any question about this, look for just a minute at the difference between the world of today and the world of 50 years ago. The technological advances have been greater than the aggregate achievement of 2,000 previous years. Social changes have been equally great. We no longer have an agrarian economy; ours is an urban civilization.

We are not concerned with building our cities; now it is a question of saving them from becoming ghettos and slums. Air pollution, water contamination, trash disposal—these are greater problems than food production. Consider what effect the advances in civil rights can have on the future of a corporation. Will a company or an industry be looked on with favor in tomorrow's society? This is part of planning, and such planning will take final shape in the corporate image. It is important to consider how much the image will be shaped by management and how much by outside circumstances.

The corporation and its image will exist in a relatively new economy —a growing, probably inflationary economy. The population of our country and the world will increase more rapidly than ever before in history. There may be problems of inflation, perhaps temporary recessions and unemployment, but total markets and incomes cannot fail to grow.

Federal, state, and local governments will have a greater effect on corporate welfare through increased control of taxation, spending, monopoly restrictions, and many other phases of business. In regard to corporate planning, what changes can be foreseen in government and what controls might be applied? What other changes in federal or state policy will affect the future of a company?

The general prosperity of the country and the specific welfare of many corporations will be closely linked with international development and trade. There can even be major changes in the medium of exchange —for example, the creation of new forms of "money." There are strong pressures for and against the restriction of imports or corporate investments in foreign countries that can be vital to international firms.

Within the domestic economy, changes will take place that can determine the direction of many companies. It is possible that more houses will be prefabricated than will be the work of local artisans. According to *The Wall Street Journal*, already one in four of all single dwellings built in 1968 was a mobile home.

Transportation of people and goods is another field that has surpassed the most optimistic forecasts and outgrown many existing facilities. Still

This chart, prepared by Walter Landor & Associates of San Francisco, illustrates the way in which an image is established by the interaction of a company and its total environment.

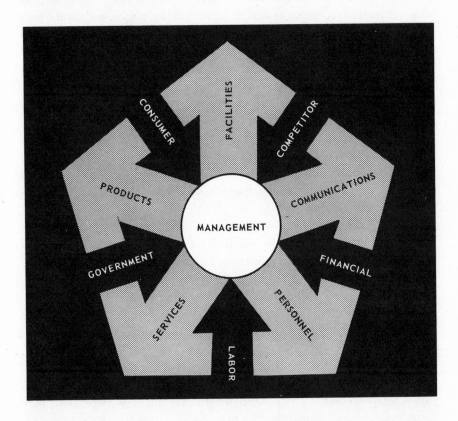

greater advances must be considered in corporate planning. Imagine the economic impact if air pollution should actually require the substitution of steam or electric autos for internal combustion engines.

Less drastic changes have their effects on many businesses, and surely the trends will not be reversed. The corner grocery became almost obsolete in the wake of supermarkets. The next development may be automatic ordering and delivery handled by computers. If a company is not using data processing, must it soon adopt it or be put out of business? Styles, fashions, and fads probably cannot be predicted electronically, but they certainly will change and, in their changes, make some firms prosperous and others bankrupt.

Decisions Based on Progress

Financing and investment decisions have always been based on possible future developments as well as on past performance, and, in the past decade, great emphasis has been placed on growth and change. Securities that have been favored in the market, as expressed in volume traded and higher prices, have often been those of scientific or technical companies or of firms affected by changes in living standards and habits.

A comprehensive study, "Investment Opportunities in a $150 Billion Market—Leisure," was issued in 1968 by Merrill Lynch, Pierce, Fenner & Smith, the largest American brokerage firm. It made a detailed analysis of the changes resulting from shorter working hours, extended vacations, earlier retirement, and greater disposable income. What these changes mean to firms in the leisure field was documented in the growth and earnings records of 74 firms.

One of many studies of new technical fields was a 1968 booklet by Roberts, Scott & Co., Inc., in which developments since 1937 were reviewed for computer science, electronics, transportation, communications, energy, oceanography, air and water pollution control, photography, chemistry, and pharmaceuticals. These developments may soon look prosaic compared with the advances in science now projected. Space has been the most spectacular area, but it may become secondary to medicine or genetics.

It is not expected that either the board of directors or the public relations department can look ahead in Orwellian fashion and know today just where its company will be in the future, but it is imperative that the effects of developments within business and throughout the world be given serious thought.

Most important are progressive management attitudes and actions. Without actual accomplishments, the company will be of little interest to the public, the financial community, or the press. Corporate growth, increased income, and contributions to the country's welfare usually result from new developments and the effective use of manpower, money, and executive and research ability. The image of a company will always be, in substantial part, the reflection of its achievements. The lily may be gilded by publicity or promotion, but it first must *be* a lily.

It is apparent that no company exists without an image, whether it has been created by the designs and efforts of the management or was arrived at involuntarily and is possibly an undesirable one. Opinions of a company may be accurate or mistaken, but the opinion will always exist. In the early history of industry, the public image was largely neglected by management and often became distorted. Mass merchandising, new methods of advertising, increased competition, and government regulations have brought corporate reputations into public view and caused executives to seek more favorable reactions.

Corporate managements are forced to realize that social changes are becoming a problem that is as important as technological developments or financial arrangements and that may be more difficult to handle. The regard in which the public holds individual corporations and business in general can depend on industry's response to these problems.

That this is the function of top management—a function that will affect the growth and earnings of individual firms—is expressed in this statement by Semon E. Knudsen, former president of Ford Motor Company, before the Economic Club of New York:

> Corporate interest in social problems is not pure altruism. The business reason for our involvement is to help create the kind of society and economic climate which will permit our companies to remain profitable over the long haul. In the shorter term, however, the exercise of social responsibility—whether it is a corporate contribution to higher education or supporting a ghetto project—is a current expense which reduces current profits.
>
> This means that one fact should be borne in mind by everyone, in or out of government and politics, and especially by those who think that any profit at all is an adequate return: The smaller the profit a company makes, the smaller the effort it can afford to make toward meeting public goals.
>
> By the same token only a thriving business firm can provide the new jobs that are needed to absorb the hard-core unemployed, which certainly must be assigned a top priority among our urgent national goals of reducing poverty and providing equal opportunity to all Americans.

Advance planning and deliberate interpretation of a company's accomplishments are the two areas in which management can make one firm look better than others. Two corporations can start from relatively equal positions in the same business, and yet one may soon greatly exceed the other in growth, earnings, and public acceptance. This is usually the result of an aggressive and progressive policy by competent management as contrasted to more conservative practices of competitors.

For example, just a few years ago, two oil companies had unusually similar positions. They were relatively small, regional, and were primarily oriented toward production rather than marketing. Both stocks were traded locally, without much movement.

The first company has grown conservatively. Its major acquisition has been a real estate holding that is being slowly developed. Other investments have been made in oil and gas production in new localities. The management of this company has been even more conservative in its relations with the financial community and the public. It has told stockholders that until accomplishments were substantially greater, no more than mandatory information would be issued. Corporate decisions have received little publicity. Earnings have improved, but not greatly.

Starting from much the same base, the second firm has become one of the fastest-growing and most active companies in the country. There have been a number of acquisitions, tenders for other corporations that resulted in substantial gains, a discovery of oil abroad, and an aggressive policy of growth. Publicity and financial public relations departments have maintained a feeling of excitement from month to month. Any move, large or small, has been reported in the press. The stock is one of the most actively traded. This has made possible further ventures and consequent public attention.

Of course, a corporate image program has not been the dominant reason for this firm's growth, nor will its policies always be the most successful. What has been demonstrated is the close relationship between management policies and image.

There are outstanding examples of companies that have grown more rapidly than their competitors and are supported by steadily increasing numbers of both customers and investors. Among them are Bank of America, now the largest bank in the country; Sears, Roebuck, first in merchandising volume; General Motors, with half the total auto sales; and Polaroid and Xerox, which are based on radically new equipment. These firms have paid close and constant attention to their images.

General Electric is recognized as one of the best examples of a favorable corporate image in industrial and consumer industries around the world and in financial circles as well. One of the firm's major decisions (made before such actions were common) was to establish a single trademark and symbol and use it on every product in a complex, diversified line. Creating General Electric's reputation involved far more than standardizing its identity. The program has not been spectacular, but it has been consistent as a result of careful preparation and implementation of all the company's contacts and communications.

The value of this established image and of the advance organization to handle any emergency was illustrated when General Electric and other companies were convicted of illegal price fixing. This was a serious situation and affected the defendant companies in different ways. General Electric was relatively unaffected, either in sales or in the opinion of the public, as represented by stock quotations. After a brief dip, General Electric bounced back into favor and became the popular blue chip it had always been.

Another pioneer corporation that made extensive changes in its operations and, eventually, in its image is General Mills. Most of the new developments came since the introduction of young management began in 1960. The company was principally involved in feeds and foods, with a high percentage in bulk flour, for which there was a declining market and profit. Although older members of the organization felt it was necessary to retain the stock-feed business, new management phased out this product line. An unprofitable venture into electronics was sold.

New promotions as well as new products have been an effective answer for General Mills. Now the corporation is recognized as growing and progressive, although no change has been made in name or identifying symbols.

Mergers Create New Identities

Many of the larger corporations are the result of a tremendous increase in the number and size of mergers and acquisitions. Among the leaders have been Litton Industries, Textron, Inc., International Telephone & Telegraph, and FMC Corporation. More recently formed conglomerates include U.S. Industries, Teledyne, Ling-Temco-Vought, Gulf & Western Industries, and Whittaker Corporation. Each has reached a volume of business several times greater than that of five years earlier, principally through acquisitions.

Banks and railroads, which have been restricted in growth by acquisitions, have become holding companies, a move that permits more flexible and diversified operations. Illinois Central Industries broadened the base of its business, as did Santa Fe Industries. Marine Midland was a pioneer in the field of expanded banking. Irving Trust Company set up Charter New York as a one-bank holding company.

Much of the emphasis upon growth has been based on projections of a larger market. Census forecasts point to an additional hundred million people in the United States within 30 years. The population explosion all over the world requires more and more jobs. At the same time, Prudential Insurance Company predicts a climb in the gross national product (the sum of all private and government spending and income) to an excess of one trillion dollars by 1971.

These advances, further spurred by inflation of prices and incomes, will require immense amounts of new capital to provide facilities for industrial production, to pay higher wages, and to finance the demands for schools, roads, hospitals, and government activities.

One hundred years ago, there was an average plant investment of only $550 for each worker; by 1968 the investment was about $20,000. This ratio continues to climb; in the petroleum industry there is a plant investment of $250,000 per employee.

In the fierce and growing competition for capital, companies that have gained the regard of shareholders and investors will have the best opportunity to market securities at reasonable rates of return. Whether the firm is growing through internal development, marketing and management efficiency, or amalgamations, it will need more and more money. As a result, corporate image programs are more frequently directed toward the financial community.

At the same time (1970) that American Telephone & Telegraph was completing the largest public financing program in history, the company was implementing a major change in its image, emphasizing its modern, progressive, and scientifically oriented policies.

In November 1968, *The Wall Street Journal* reported that the demand for financial public relations personnel was rapidly increasing. The *Journal* quoted an employment agent as saying, "the old product publicity boys are dead. Companies now want guys who practically sleep with the security analysts." The growth of conglomerate firms, the merger boom, and the increased stress on disclosure of financial affairs are credited with spurring this job boom. At the same time, general public regard must be maintained for the successful marketing of products as well as the creation of new investors.

The interest of the financial community has been sought by companies desiring mergers and acquisitions, and these firms make up a growing segment of large and small businesses. When directors and stockholders of a company are asked to sell or merge their holdings with another firm, they must be convinced that the union is desirable. If they believe that the buying corporation is progressive, capable, and potentially more profitable, they will be disposed to approve its offer. Conversely, if firms that are on the market look good to the investment community, there will be more potential buyers who offer higher prices.

There can be a pyramiding effect of acquisitions and the accompanying announcements. If the reception is favorable, the corporation becomes an investment favorite. It is actively traded by mutual funds and individuals. This trading draws attention, which, in turn, invites further amalgamations. However, there is always the possibility that the newly created company may not do as well as hoped, thus promoting adverse feelings in investors.

When a corporation plans to grow by taking over other firms through the exchange of stocks, it is almost essential that it have a favorable price-earnings ratio. This means that the price of its stock must be a high multiple of current earnings per share. Until a few years ago, the stocks of major corporations were usually quoted in the Dow-Jones averages from 10 to 12 and occasionally up to 20 times earnings. Corporations that are actively traded have ranged up to 80 or even 100 times earnings, based on expectations of continued rapid growth. It is obvious that a company with a price-earnings ratio of 60 is in a favorable position to exchange with a firm that is quoted at 10 or 15 times earnings. It may have been necessary for the acquired company to sell out, or management may believe that combined growth will justify the difference in price, but there is no doubt that the seller is at a disadvantage.

Widely used methods of acquisition have been the issuance of convertible bonds or stock warrants, which presumably give the seller a fair return and the future option of owning stock in the parent corporation. It is again obvious that the management of the selling firm must have a favorable opinion of its purchaser if it accepts such securities.

It is becoming widely recognized, incidentally, that merger is not always a satisfactory answer. Where the result is not happy, an effort is usually made to carry it off rather than dissolve the union, but there have been a number of corporate divorces. Booz, Allen & Hamilton Inc., estimates that out of 120 firms that merged in 1968, only 64 would do it again. Jerome S. Hollender, of Shearson, Hammill & Co., says that of 100 mergers, only 41 exceeded or equaled expectations, in 34 there was some disappointment, and in 25 there was extreme disappointment.

Federal, state, and local governments increasingly affect business in general and individual companies. There are greater regulation of monopoly and more challenges to proposed mergers. The SEC has issued stronger rules regarding the disclosure of financial information and provided greater protection for investors.

Government is in competition with private industry in such areas as electric power generation. Investments in foreign nations are controlled, and foreign securities are taxed. Federal and state bureaus are involved in labor disputes, employment practices, regulation of utility rates, control of air and water pollution, product safety, and advertising—in hundreds of large and small business activities.

Contact with government and development of a favorable image are receiving increased attention from corporate executives. Some firms have set up special committees or departments to plan and prepare for government contacts, including hearings and industry investigations as well as specific corporate problems. If a corporation is at odds with government, it may seek public support, even public appeals to elected representatives. If the company has established a favorable image in advance of the trouble, it will be in a better position to gain such support.

Long-Range Planning

The corporate image should be as much a part of long-range planning as research, marketing, or finance. As it is a reflection of all the activities of the company, it should be considered in relation to these activities. No company exists without an image. If the image is ignored during the planning stage, the true picture of the company may be distorted. If production, research, finance, marketing, and other major functions of management are the building blocks with which the corporation is constructed, the corporate image is the facade that is seen by everyone.

In many organizations, the importance of a favorable image has been recognized only in recent years. Corporations that saw the advantage of public recognition early in their history and consistently worked on a public relations program have usually been standout performers. This is not hard to understand, because the same foresight that planned successful development in research, marketing, and management created and maintained the proper reflection of these achievements.

The importance of identity as a foundation for a favorable image has been realized by many leading firms that have made changes in recent years. David Rockefeller, chairman of The Chase Manhattan Bank, has been quoted as follows:

> Every company has an opportunity to project a corporate identity that is clear, forceful, and unmistakably individual. When the identity scheme is artistic and a *planned one,* so that each element is blended with the others, the result can be quite striking.

The corporate image is one means of creating a personality, of offsetting the feeling that all industrial companies are cold and impersonal. On this point, Dr. Frank Stanton, president of Columbia Broadcasting System, has said:

> I think there are few needs greater for the modern, large-scale corporation than the need for a broad public awareness of its personality—its sense of values. Increasingly, I think modern corporations are recognizing the high cost of impersonality. Everything we produce at the Columbia Broadcasting System, including our own printed advertising, reports, documents, and promotion, is carefully considered from the viewpoint of the image we have of ourselves as a vigorous, public-spirited, profitable, modern enterprise. We give the most careful attention to all aspects of design. We believe that we should not only be progressive, but look progressive. We aim at excellence in all the arts, including the art of self-expression.

In the annual report of Boise Cascade Corporation, the president, R. V. Hansberger, states the viewpoint of a growing firm:

> Over the years at Boise Cascade, we have developed an attitude about people that has proved to be, for us at least, highly effective. This attitude is that people are most productive when they are regarded as individuals and provided with an environment which encourages them to do the company's work in their own individual way. We have worked hard to maintain this "state of mind" about our people in spite of the growing size of the corporation. In this way we think it has been possible to blend the advantages of size and financial strength with the advantages of smallness, such as flexibility and individuality.

Many modern corporations have substantially changed their original image. The need for introduction of a new image is expressed by Robert S. Ingersoll, chairman of Borg-Warner Corp. He said,

> We want to make the name Borg-Warner, and the quality and integrity the name stands for, well known in the business community, and at least recognizable to the consumer public. It seems obvious to us that our company can benefit by selling the universally respected Borg-Warner name along with the division names. This is a problem of mutual support that should redound to the benefit of all of us.

To realize the need for a revised image will not necessarily produce a favorable result, any more than an expressed plan of technical research will create desirable new products. A favorable image comes from careful planning based on research and consistent work toward the established objectives. In some firms, such planning and work have been inconsistent and often short term. The corporate image has been confused with publicity, which is too often measured by the number of clippings.

Corporations that do not offer consumer products may direct a disproportionate share of attention to the financial community without considering the effect of public opinion. The reverse has been true in other firms that have sought consumer recognition but overlooked attention to financial and investment areas. Either error may result from delegation of responsibility to subordinate departments instead of operating the program at the executive level.

Some executives may have reached their position through production, financial, or legal channels, and in some cases have had little contact with marketing, advertising, and public relations. Such executives may tend to shift these functions to others or not include them in long-range planning.

Evaluation of the image and any attempt to make it representative and appealing must be functions of top-level management if action is to be effective. The decision to revise physical identity can involve many of the people in an organization and represent an important item in the budget. A change can affect volume and profit, the enlistment of personnel, and other vital factors in the success of the business.

Conversely, unless the program for improvement of the image has the strong support of top management, there is little chance that it will be successful. The proposed changes must result from a firm conviction of the executives and the board that changes are needed.

The need for a revised image may arise out of important changes in the business itself. Mergers, product development, moves into new markets—such changes can make the overall image obsolete. The firm may have started with an incorrect image or acquired one over the years. Some boards and executives find it difficult to realize how much their image needs correction. They do not see that a slipping image is apparent to aggressive competitors, customers, and eventually to investors.

The Cumulative Effect

The same executive leadership that is essential for the creation of the improved corporate image is essential for its maintenance. Obviously, a company cannot gain acceptance for a new posture by simply announcing, "Look at me, I'm progressive today." No matter how much effort is involved and money spent, there will be potential customers and investors who won't notice, or won't care, for a long time. A successful program must pick up momentum as it goes along. Everyone in the firm must contribute to a drive that is fueled and guided by management. When employees, dealers, customers, competitors, and investors start talking about the improvement of a company, a brighter image has been established.

The corporate image is, among other things, the voice on the telephone, the response to customer complaints, the colors of company buildings and signs, the difficulty or ease of opening packages, reports of sales and earnings, the price of the company stock—all the products, properties, employees, advertising, publicity, and literature. Some impressions are of interest to only a particular group but, in the aggregate, they form the image of the corporation.

The corporate identity is usually built around a name or a symbol that is widely associated with products and promotion materials. The company wants to have its name and emblems widely known and pleasantly associated with its products, business dealings, and shares in its ownership.

Among the means used to implement a new image are advertising, annual and interim reports, community relations, labor relations, employee indoctrination, industry campaigns and activities, motion pictures, speakers, product packaging, meetings with members of the financial community, shareholder cooperation, and possibly most important of all, word-of-mouth endorsement. The most effective means of creating a new image or improving an old one are discussed in the following chapters. Even a cas-

Sharp contrasts are shown between earlier corporate identities and modern designs for these major companies. (*Courtesy Lippincott & Margulies*)

ual look at the image now presented by hundreds of corporations, in contrast to their posture of a few years ago, shows how rapidly changes have taken place.

Sometimes the image of a large company can be improved without changes in product lines or organization framework. Chrysler Corporation was getting into trouble with the public's acceptance of the firm and its products, with the morale of the dealer organization, its appeal to investors, and the direction in which management was headed. As an added handicap, Chrysler's identity had been presented—or permitted to appear —in so many physical forms that it could not look other than fuzzy. When Lynn Townsend took over management in 1961, one of his high priority programs was the establishment of a more definite image. This was to be a top-level campaign, and he is reported to have declared that nobody else was to touch it.

After checking and confirming the company's position and problems and considering a number of suggested programs, Chrysler adopted the "pentastar" as the identity symbol around which the new image campaign was to be built. All physical presentations of the company and its divisions were made to employ the star. In the past, there had been so many different appearances of the company and product names that at times more than one style was used in a single advertisement.

The entire organization was imbued with the necessity of presenting to the public the image of a revived, progressive company. Since the new program was begun, each of the divisions has had more aggressive advertising and promotion, some of it definitely slanted to a youthful audience, but all presentations have been closely linked to the central image.

Options Are Available

Among the possible changes to be considered are these:

1. The existing image may be modified or modernized without a major change in name or symbol. Uniformity can be achieved, and a sense of progress indicated.

2. A completely new image may be created, based on a new name or symbol. There may or may not be some continuation of the previous identity. There must be a strong program to establish quickly a previously unknown image.

3. An identity may be simplified by using initials as the corporate

identity. IBM, SCM, ITT, and other firms have made this change as their activities extended far beyond the original area.

4. Symbols and newly acquired subsidiary or division names may be abandoned and all promotion given to the corporate name. This is a definite simplification and standardization.

5. Long or hyphenated names may be shortened or combined.

The selection of one of these options will depend on the long-range objectives of the entire program, which should be set up only after careful consideration.

When the fundamental objectives have been established, the promotion targets will become apparent. If the program is being changed primarily to influence bankers and investors, emphasis will be given to financial public relations. Or the corporation may be more concerned with public attitudes that could affect control of resources or regulation of earnings rates.

A timber company seeking contracts for selective cutting in national forests wants to forestall organized opposition from conservationists or sportsmen. An oil company with plans for offshore drilling will seek to show that beaches will not be polluted. Location of an industrial plant near a residential area can become controversial. Normally these are short-term problems, although possible air and water contamination are questions of continuing responsibility. In the longer view, most corporations are concerned with sales of products at profitable prices, employment of competent workers, approval of the financial community, and possibly the acquisition of other firms.

Companies that once served only industrial markets may have entered consumer fields only to find that their image does not fit the new surroundings. Highly technical organizations were content with an obscure image as long as they served only a limited number of customers; when their markets widened, it became important to establish a clearer identity. Older firms were often lax about the presentation of their identity. They permitted the company name and symbols to appear in varied forms—and thus lacked simple and standardized corporate appearances.

Identity Problems

Management policies for the identification of new companies in a diversified corporation are guided by the degree to which new divisions are integrated. One question is whether it is preferable to bring all the acquisitions under the parent roof or to leave them relatively independent.

Textron was one of the first and largest firms to branch out in many directions. From a base of textile companies, more than 60 acquisitions were made, ranging from cement and electronics to table silver and chickens. Textron lets its divisions and subsidiaries operate their own businesses with financial and management assistance if needed.

With a different objective, Electronic Specialty Company took over 22 firms in 10 years. In most cases, these were companies in one of its three principal lines of business. So far as possible, production and marketing were consolidated.

If the average investor were asked what corporation includes car rentals, home building, hotels, cellulose and other basic products, insurance and finance, as well as a broad line of communications and electronic products, he might not guess International Telephone & Telegraph Company. Once primarily engaged in international communications, ITT lost six plants and two phone systems by expropriation. Then, under new management, the company grew and diversified rapidly until only a small part of its business was either international or telephone. The corporate name was retained, but all identification is now ITT, and a consistent campaign promotes knowledge of this symbol.

Food Machinery Company was founded in 1928 by the merger of two agricultural and canning equipment firms. It grew through the acquisition of 30 or more companies, most of them closely related. When it entered the area of agricultural chemicals, the firm became Food Machinery & Chemical Corporation, but after the acquisition of American Viscose and Link-Belt Company and the development of many product lines, even that identity was too restrictive. Management simplified its name to FMC Corporation, permitting a certain ambiguity to cover many industries.

These are only a few examples of the thousands of corporations that have established new or modernized images in the last few years. Each company has its individual situation and its unique opportunities and problems.

2

The Advantages
of a Favorable Image

THE long-range rationale for a favorable corporate image is that such an image produces a climate conducive to growth and improved earnings. The advantages gained reflect sound planning by management, and the corporate image program becomes a valuable part of overall operations. Among these advantages, aside from increased sales and profits, are better relations with customers and the government, ability to enlist good distributors and dealers as well as desirable middle- and top-level personnel, protection against tenders and take-overs, and attraction of possible acquisitions and of new investors. Last but not least, a company gains a positive attitude from the general public and wins the loyalty and enthusiasm of its employees.

Not every corporation will be interested in all these possible advantages, and most will consider one or two more important than the others. The value of certain advantages will be clear upon analysis of the corporation's existing position and its future plans.

Image Does Affect Sales and Earnings

Confirmation of the theory that an established, favorable corporate image does contribute to sales and earnings is found in a two-year study by the advertising agency Batten, Barton, Durstine & Osborn, Inc.

Two companies in each of four industries were paired, one with a substantially higher price-earnings ratio for its common stock. In-home interviews were held with men and women who had incomes of $10,000 or more in a broad geographical sample. One conclusion was quickly apparent:

> In essence, a company is judged by the consumer on the basis of how well he thinks that company performs its principal mission; and a company gains an increment of public approval for its "good works" only if it is first considered to be providing good products or services at a fair price.

Without exception, the companies with higher price-earnings ratios were rated higher on all these points:

1. It is always improving its product lines or introducing new products.
2. It is a very profitable company.
3. The public would believe management's statements in a labor dispute.
4. The public would be more willing to buy that company's products than those of other companies.
5. The public would be willing to pay a higher price for its products.
6. The public is very familiar with this company.
7. It cares about the public interest.
8. Its concern with the public interest improves its standing as an investment.
9. Its concern with the public interest increases public belief in management's statements during labor disputes.

For further evidence BBD&O conducted a quantitative test on 22 companies in the top 150 corporations, picking 12 firms thought to be well known and 10 that were not so well known. Interviews with a national sample of respondents showed that the well-known corporations were familiar to 96 percent, the less well-known ones to 51 percent.

A close correlation was established between knowledge of products or services and belief that the company "cares." Almost without exception, ratings were two to three times as high for the well-known firms on credibility, willingness to pay more for products, and investment merit. The report summarized:

If customers think that a company cares about the public interest:
1. They are more likely to believe its statements on controversial subjects, such as proxy fights and labor disputes.
2. They think its products are of higher quality.
3. They are willing to pay more for its products.
4. They will buy new products from this company more readily than they would from other companies.
5. They think the company is a good investment.
6. The company's stock tends to suffer less decline in an adverse market.
7. The company tends to enjoy a higher price-earnings ratio.

Buying Habits Are Strong

To most people, the use of a product or service becomes a habit that grows stronger with time, so long as nothing occurs to cause dissatisfaction. People set patterns of shopping: They go to the same stores and often to the same salespeople, use the same bank, barber, or beauty shop, take their cars to the same service station. Certain brands become favorites, and only a strong appeal from a rival brand or an unfortunate experience with the favorite will cause a change in selections.

There is a difference in the loyalty given different products. Auto manufacturers expect a high percentage of owners to buy the same make again or at least to give it first consideration. Men and women who are satisfied with a brand of shirts or shoes will usually look for that maker's name when they shop. In spite of the appeals of "specials" and other inducements by competitors, a good many foods consistently hold a high percentage of the total market.

In contrast, consumer surveys have shown that car owners see little difference in gasolines, in spite of the heavy promotion campaigns. They are more interested in a convenient location, in the service given, or in a lower price.

Because shopping and service habits can be established early in family life, manufacturers and retailers work hard to gain favor with young people. In recent years, more and more products and services have been aimed at the young. Financial institutions offer family budget books, plans for owning a home, and other inducements. Brokerage firms have seminars for beginning investors, banks extend student loans, insurance companies plan programs to fit young family growth. Brides start sets of their silver and porcelain patterns, and usually their selection is based on brands seen in their parents' homes.

Among national merchandisers, changes are reflected in business growth and the acceptance of securities. J. C. Penney was for many years considered a chain of relatively small, neighborhood stores that featured products of good value but little style and limited lines. Now Penney's advertisements claim competitive styling, the stores have expanded to sell appliances as well as soft goods, and credit is available. The firm may not have lost all of its former image, but it does present a new face to customers and to investors.

Montgomery Ward followed conservative policies for many years at a time when other mass merchandisers were expanding as rapidly as possible. As a result it grew slowly and its stock was stagnant. Under new management, growth was launched and a new identity set up by the merger with Container Corporation.

Aggressive advertising and promotion had two goals—to attract younger and more style-conscious buyers and to identify the new name, Marcor, as an active, profitable company. Full pages in financial publications announced the merger, and a continuing campaign reminds investors and brokers of Marcor. This has been one of the more pronounced changes in image among retail organizations.

An established and favorable identity is practically essential in scientific, technical, and other fields where performance is the criterion. Contracts for huge projects go to experienced firms as a rule. Critical parts for space vehicles or scientific instruments are ordered from well-known organizations. It is true that performance has to be established before the favorable image, but these corporations work constantly to maintain their recognized position.

Reputation Attracts Personnel

Some aspects of an image create little comment, but the reputation of a company as an employer becomes quickly recognized. Some firms are considered a good place to work while others are not. For creative, ambitious men and women, immediate income may not be the primary consideration, because they are looking for advancement, recognition, association with success, and pleasant working conditions.

If a company is successful, growing, recognized as a leader, and steadily seeking new fields to conquer, it attracts desirable employees. Insiders are quickly aware of the firm's position, often before outsiders see changes or developments. What they say, in and out of the organization, is important for industrial relations departments and management.

In contrast, many key people in one of the aerospace companies feel insecure because some programs are discarded and others started on short notice. This has resulted in shifts of personnel and loss of position and advancement. The changing policies of the firm have also been affected in its relation to the financial community.

The solution to one problem may create others. The question of who will survive after each merger is definitely unsettling and creates ill will among those who are demoted or dismissed.

A case of two mergers involving the same company is an example of divergent results. In the first merger, places were made for all the acquired personnel who wanted to stay through a real effort to bring these men into responsible positions. The result was a big, happy family, but one in which there were too many chiefs for the size of the business.

Later, this company was absorbed by a much larger organization, and this time a principal objective was to cut costs by eliminating duplicate functions and personnel. Many employees were given the option of moving or leaving; others just received their separation pay. There was little doubt that eventually the efficiency of the corporation was improved and expenses reduced, but during this process the headquarters city rang with the complaints of the dispossessed.

This is a situation that faces many managements, and probably the solution is to put the best possible face on what has to be done. Somewhat the same conditions exist when plants are moved or closed, a problem that is discussed at greater length in another chapter.

One of the most frustrating situations for key employees is when changes should be made and are being discussed, but just don't happen.

Firms with older managers who are more interested in preserving their retirement rights than in progress can be throttled this way. Many aspiring executives shun family firms in the belief that only the heirs and relatives will ever reach top management positions.

When a company runs into adversity and its image goes downhill, it becomes more and more difficult to attract outstanding personnel. One national drug company spent at least a year seeking a research director. The salary and benefits were attractive, but qualified scientists felt that the opportunity for successful development was lacking. Give a dog a bad name, and nobody wants to get into the doghouse with it.

Firms seeking hard-to-find scientific and technical personnel run advertisements that feature their projects and accomplishments rather than just name salaries. These firms and their projects are usually well known to qualified applicants.

A comprehensive study was made of the responses to national employment advertisements in such publications as *Scientific American* and *Aviation Week* and the correspondence that developed from the responses. In addition to checking the effectiveness of various appeals and methods of follow-up, the survey classified the expressed wishes of applicants. Salaries and benefits were about the same and were not an issue.

Opportunities for advancement and interesting work were given top priority by most men. Certain living conditions, such as a good climate, proximity to technical universities, and good schools for children, were needs often expressed, and offering tuition for advanced education was a good inducement.

Most of the applicants knew a good deal about the companies and their projects. Information about future company plans was requested by many, particularly those seeking upper-level jobs. At the time of this study, stability of employment was a minor consideration, as most of the firms were constantly seeking personnel and the overall market for scientific and technical people was growing.

Size and Trend Factors

Success has a tendency to pyramid and so does adversity, so the fortunes of a company are inclined to continue on an up or down trend far beyond the time when the causes cease to exist. If an auto maker has an unpopular series or two, it will take time for customers to recognize the

merits of new models. This has been shown in the swings that take place in the share of the total market.

The enthusiastic reception of a new product or service will have a greater effect than the impact of that one offering. Both customers and investors tend to expect further success and to go along with winners. If the credit card of a bank becomes popular, its use will induce people to use other services of that bank.

The same feeling of loyalty—really a desire to be identified with a leading product—applies to distributors and dealers. If the product is a franchise, investors are more apt to choose one that is established rather than a new venture. If it is a product that shares store space with competitors, the dealer wants it to be favorably known so that his offerings will be recognized and accepted by consumers. He wants to put up the banner of widely advertised, widely accepted products.

In the sense that it represents the ability, experience, and integrity of a corporation, the importance of the image becomes greater as the size of the transaction grows. A buyer may not demand that a fractional-horse-power motor carry a major brand name, but when construction of a nuclear power plant or a contract for jet engines is under consideration, the established company gets preference.

An investor may be willing to buy ten or even a hundred shares of stock in a company he does not know well on the recommendation of a broker, but a fund manager will look carefully at the record before he includes 50,000 shares in the portfolio. Stock holdings in the larger and older mutual funds and the portfolios of foundations and universities are often equivalent to a list of the leading corporations.

Suppliers and service organizations also want to work with successful companies, and their assistance can be substantial. With other conditions equal, banks would rather lend to a well-known firm than to a newcomer. When there are shortages of materials, established firms get better service from suppliers. Price is not always the key factor, any more than salary is for prospective employees.

One of the real problems of certain corporations is how to avoid arousing the public's resentment. A company that has a broad monopoly, such as a public utility or a transportation firm, is often the target of complaints and even active dislike. The public is inclined to notice the failings in service rather than the benefits. At one time, the managements of utilities and other firms with a full or partial monopoly were notorious

In three-quarters of a century the AT&T bell has been changed and modernized along with the company's image.

| 1889 | 1900 | 1921 |

| 1939 | 1964 | 1969 |

in their disregard of public relations. Some still appear to be, but most now have an enlightened point of view and act accordingly.

Probably the longest and certainly the largest public relations campaign is that of the American Telephone & Telegraph Company. The only aim of its advertising and public relations activities is to make friends of its customers, as it has nothing but service to sell, at least to the general public. "Ma Bell" resulted in the image of a warm, humane service organization and—coincidentally—gave AT&T the greatest number of shareholders of any American corporation. Now the company is making a broad change in its image, identification, and even its company colors. It seeks to be considered innovative and scientific as a result of its achievements and contributions to defense and space.

It is a challenging and sometimes frightening prospect to realize that a corporation, or even an industry, can quickly fall into disfavor with the public, customers, and investors. The support given an industry when it is attacked is often weak and quickly dissipated. To say that the public is fickle is an old cliché, but it is also a fact that comes to haunt business just as it does politicians or entertainers.

What Ralph Nader has done to the automobile industry's image could hardly have been imagined ten years ago. The drug industry is under attack from several directions and looks bruised if not beaten. More than one company is being investigated for air or water pollution. Natural-resource industries are subject to periods of attack. Manufacturers of defense materials are charged with complicity to increase spending for armaments.

There is no doubt that many charges and attacks are promoted by relatively small groups, but they do get coverage in the news media and have generated some consumer support. It is not expected that any program can fully prevent unwarranted harassment, but a well-organized policy and continued attention by an alert staff can do much to counteract these blemishes on the corporate image.

Catastrophe—The Test of an Image

The value of a favorable image and the necessity of an organized plan to protect it can be seen when a real catastrophe hits a corporation. How a company can come through months of serious trouble with its image unimpaired and ready for strong advances is shown by the case of Cutter Laboratories in Berkeley, California.

Several years ago, this firm and others prepared and tested polio vaccine under government instructions. Use of this vaccine caused attacks and these cases were followed by large damage suits. It was later established that there was no negligence on the part of Cutter, but this proof had to wait until new tests, discovered and developed *after* the vaccine was released, showed that neither government nor Cutter scientists were able to find any infective polio virus in the original vaccine.

The financial strain on the company could have been even worse if negligence had been proved against Cutter. Even more disastrous would have been the blackening of the company's reputation. A drug company's life depends on its reputation for the quality and purity of its products.

There was widespread alarm when it was disclosed that children in certain areas supplied by Cutter Laboratories had contracted polio after vaccination. First news reports assumed carelessness in preparation of the vaccine. It was essential that the medical profession support Cutter while the situation was being investigated.

Cutter was fortunate that it had worked for and earned first, a reputation as a thoroughly scientific firm, and, second, feelings of warm friendship with all its business contacts. This friendship was more than a passive acceptance of the company—it was a remarkable atmosphere, which reflected the personal wishes of the Cutter family. Similar policies existed for suppliers, outside agencies serving the firm, and for doctors and hospitals. Sales representatives were taught that they represented the company as well as its products. When part of the labor force struck Cutter along with other plants in the area, the company kept pickets supplied with hot coffee.

Dr. Robert Cutter, president, issued a statement and asked physicians and hospital administrators for help. His request resulted in a stream of letters expressing confidence in the company. These letters were given wide publicity. As the situation quieted down, material about Cutter was sent to editors of medical, hospital, drug, veterinarian, and ranching publications, including editorial comment from writers who had taken time to look into the facts. It was pointed out that Cutter was making no claims, only asking the profession to "wait and see." When the government report cleared Cutter of blame, meetings were held and releases written to every medium to review the problem as it existed and how it had been handled.

Months later, when both medical and financial settlements had been completed, the company brought together news representatives and opinion leaders to thank them for their cooperation and to give them an accounting of the handling of the campaign.

Two things are significant in the Cutter story and that of other companies that have weathered such storms: (1) A well-established and favorable image makes possible reasonable understanding and treatment of emergency news, and (2) a carefully organized program is essential.

Some one person must be appointed to carry out the program and the policy of the corporation in any situation should be established. Normally, it is best to tell the complete story, holding back nothing. Procedures for writing releases by competent personnel and approval by specified executives should be understood.

The Case of Union Oil Company

A problem that aroused unusual community and government concern, as well as that of the financial world, faced Union Oil Company. Union was the operating firm for a group of oil companies that joined in underwater drilling near Santa Barbara, California. A large leak developed from which oil spread into the harbors of Santa Barbara, Ventura, and Oxnard and threatened to extend to beaches near Los Angeles. There was extensive damage to property and a possible threat to marine life.

The corporation took immediate steps to check the spread of oil and put large crews to work cleaning up the beaches and harbors. State and community organizations rushed to sue Union Oil and to urge that undersea drilling be stopped. The Department of the Interior issued an order to halt operations and started a survey of possible controls and precautions to prevent similar accidents.

Before a congressional committee, the president, Fred L. Hartley, was misquoted as having made an unfortunate remark about the furore over the death of a few birds in contrast to the silence over other critical situations in the nation. In an emotional atmosphere, this was magnified and distorted through wide publicity until Union Oil decided the situation required action. This was done through a large newspaper advertisement that began, "Please, Let's Set the Record Straight." Copy cited the correct statement and the context of the remark.

This counteraction only marked the start of seemingly endless trouble —billions of dollars in damage suits from communities and the state of California and a series of articles, editorials, and letters that condemned offshore drilling in general and Union Oil in particular.

President Hartley issued bulletins to all employees and to the press, stating the company's version of the situation. The first said,

> We have marshalled our skills and our people in full cooperation with agencies of federal, state, and local governments in working toward a common goal of control and cleanup. More than a score of boats, several airplanes, miles of wooden and plastic booms, thousands of bales of straw, dozens of vacuum trucks, dump trucks and bulldozers, and more than 400 men are engaged in cleanup operations on land and sea. In addition, on my orders 16 of our top research people were dispatched to Santa Barbara last week to establish a bird cleaning and care center and are cooperating with the Department of Fish and Game in cleaning

and caring for fowl that may have encountered oil. They have been very successful in their efforts and you may rest assured, contrary to what has been reported in the media, we are not taking this matter lightly or callously.

It is well nigh impossible to say how deeply we regret this accident. We have operated at all times [in accordance] with procedures approved by the federal regulatory authority. What happened is, to our knowledge, very rare in the long history of offshore oil exploration and production.

Neither the community organizations nor the press let the controversy quiet down, and weeks later another channel of communication was opened in defense of the industry. Henry Morrison, vice-president and general manager of the Western Oil and Gas Association, described in the *Los Angeles Times* the Association's studies of damage to marine life and the efforts of the industry to clean up the beaches. The Association engaged Dr. Wheeler J. North, marine biologist from the California Institute of Technology, to head an interim study of immediate effects on plants and animals and made a $220,000 grant to the University of Southern California for a year-long survey.

Both protest and publicity continued, and there is little chance that all phases of this situation will be made known for several years. Union Oil is quietly explaining its actions and its position and reserving comment on the legal suits, but it has little option other than waiting out the situation.

IBM Answers Monopoly Charges

Early in 1969, IBM was charged with monopolistic practices by the federal government and sued for restraint of trade by Control Data Corporation and Data Processing Financial and General Corporation. Here was a strong attack on one of the leading corporations, for many years a favorite of investors and held in the portfolio of more funds than any other stock. IBM was a company with an image of continued success, backed by spectacular growth and steadily rising security prices.

IBM felt that earlier suggestions that there was a lack of competition in the computer industry were unjustified and that the suits were part of this pattern. To explain the company's ideas of monopoly, large-scale advertising was used. The basic ad was headed:

Has IBM spoiled the computer business for others?
Let's look at the record

Copy read as follows:

> Believe some of the things you hear about the computer industry today
> and you might conclude that IBM has sapped the health of the industry
> and monopolized it.
>
> As some would have you see it, the industry has been stifled in its
> growth. They would have you believe that competition has been inhib-
> ited, that no one other than IBM can make money in it, that innovation
> is sluggish, that technological advancement in the industry has been
> held back.
>
> This would indeed be dangerous—*if the charges were true.* The facts
> tell another story. They make it clear that the computer industry—one
> of the fastest growing in the United States—is one of the nation's
> healthiest, most open-ended, competitive industries, one of the most
> innovative and progressive. They make it clear that IBM has not hin-
> dered the growth of competition in the industry.

The advertisement went on to speak of monopoly power and defined
a monopoly as an industry where innovation is throttled, where there is
no price competition, and where the interests of the customer are subordinated. It stated:

> These are hardly the characteristics of the computer industry that is
> alleged to be a "monopoly" of IBM. But let the facts of the industry
> speak for themselves. They tell it better than we could.

The copy continued to discuss each of the considerations listed as factors of monopoly, for example, limited opportunities for growth:

> The multibillion dollar computer industry, just a raw idea 20 years ago,
> today has attracted more than 60 manufacturers of systems, another
> 4,000 companies dealing in related equipment, support, and services.

Further sections named the large corporations in the computer industry and the entry into this business of new firms from aerospace and
other fields. The industry prediction of a 20 percent growth per year was
quoted. Another section reported the tens of thousands of firms in all

parts of the country offering supplies, support, and service to the 60,000 computer users. Charges against the corporation were repudiated, and it was concluded that the industry was in a better position because of IBM's expansion than it would otherwise have been.

This case is a good example of a strong response to serious charges; the company is convinced that its position is fully justified. The fact that the response was made by a corporation with a favorable image gave it a strength that would not otherwise have existed.

An Image Affects Market Transactions

Companies that are the target of tender offers or other take-over attempts, or that publicly discuss possible mergers that are never completed, are like a soccer ball in an active game, moving rapidly in one direction after another without reaching a goal and receiving a good many kicks along the way. If and when the situation is cleared, there is urgent necessity to look at the score and see what can be done.

Over a period of years, Allis-Chalmers was reported to be joining one or another corporation. Some of the applicants made merger offers; others accumulated stock in an effort to gain control. During this time, the stock market did not treat Allis-Chalmers kindly. The government, through the FTC, acted to block a proposed union with White Consolidated Industries.

Management of Allis-Chalmers resisted White's bid for control and advertisements in financial media announced the firm's intention to go it alone. One advertisement admitted problems, "After Major Surgery," but went on to claim a program of profitability: "Allis-Chalmers Now Is a New Company." Both firms took to print to defend their positions. White mailed proxy material to Allis-Chalmers stockholders, recommending the election of nine current White directors to the twelve-man board of Allis-Chalmers.

To combat a take-over bid by National Union Electric Corporation, National Presto Industries, Inc. resorted to humor in its advertising. The ad quoted from the NUE prospectus:

"World's First Comic Prospectus"
"Read About 'Funny Money' "

"How Emerson Turned the Profit Corner and other Factual but Hilarious Stuff"

The proposed exchange offer "must be classified as a joke," contended M. S. Cohen, Presto's president. He told stockholders, "If you are a Presto stockholder, it's your company, your earnings, your potential, your cash. Who gets the last laugh is up to you."

The aura of success—an image of growth and profits plus the potential of further progress—is reflected in the securities of a corporation. Among the measures used by the financial community are the price-earnings ratio of the stock, its rise in price, the volume traded, the number of institutions holding the stock, the growing number of shareholders, and the earnings trends. In turn, these values are assigned according to the increased sales volume, the rate and continuation of profit margins, the number of successful acquisitions, the introduction of successful new products, and the expansion into wider domestic or foreign markets.

For any corporation that plans to grow through merger or acquisition, the price-earnings ratio is an essential consideration if amalgamations are to be made by exchange of securities rather than for cash. An extremely high price-earnings ratio, and an upward climb in price over a long period, are symbols of the esteem with which investors hold a few spectacularly successful corporations. Only unusual growth patterns can earn this recognition.

An extreme example of the effect of widely separated price-earnings ratios, reflecting to some extent the images of two corporations, was the attempted take-over of Collins Radio Company by a smaller Dallas company, Electronic Data Systems Corporation.

As analyzed in *The Wall Street Journal* of May 9, 1969, Electronic Data Systems, with annual sales of $8 million, made a tender offer for Collins Radio, with $440 million in sales. The opportunity arose because Collins stock was then selling at 12 times earnings and had dropped 50 percent from its high, while EDS was priced about 300 times earnings and had climbed from its initial offering at $16.50 to $40 in six months.

According to the *Wall Street Journal* report, one securities analyst blamed Collins' erratic earnings and its "incredible ineptitude in telling its story to Wall Street." One of the Collins executives was quoted as saying, "It looks like the offer may force us to combine with someone or face being taken over." Chairman Arthur Collins opposed immediate action and refused to negotiate with EDS and, at least for the time, averted a take-over bid. When the tender offer was withdrawn, one official commented that "Collins shareholders just didn't want to give up what they had, when they didn't know what they'd get in return."

Stock volume traded is not necessarily an indication of investor favor, but a high rate of exchange can and does contribute to higher prices and certainly is a measure of public attention. In recent years, the greatest trading volume has marked corporations that are growing by acquisition as well as internal development. The interest of traders has been so great that, in some cases, four or five times as many shares change hands in a year as there are shares outstanding.

The number of institutions, such as mutual and pension funds, universities, foundations, and insurance companies, that hold shares in a corporation is another measure of its image. These organizations report their holdings at periodic intervals. Historically, institutions confined their investments to blue chips; however, in recent years, new types of funds are active traders, looking for relatively quick gains. Their holdings are often in new issues, sometimes traded over the counter, usually of limited size and subject to extended movements as they are bought and sold.

With all the changes that have taken place in the size and nature of many corporations, stocks that were quiet for years have become active while former favorites have declined. This changing interest does not depend solely on existing sales and earnings. It represents opinions on future developments that may be outside the control of a corporation—war or peace, inflation, international frictions, changes in the supply of money, changes in governments, or other major considerations that can directly affect a specific segment of business.

An increased number of shareholders is often desirable for a corporation, and the attraction of these investors depends to some extent on the firm's projection of its image. The stock exchanges require a certain number of shareholders for a stock to be listed. During recent years a growing number of firms have moved from unlisted to listed positions. Distribution of stock over a larger number of investors usually gives greater market stability, as the stock is not so subject to the movement of large blocks or other conditions of a thin market.

Added shareholders can recommend other investors and possibly some customers for the firm's products. However, a large number of small shareholders can be expensive in the servicing of dividends, proxy notices, annual reports, and other required communications, so the multiplication of investors can become a mixed blessing.

Can an Image Influence Government Action?

Just how much effect a reputation or image can have on governmental bodies is hard to determine, but the different treatment afforded different companies under similar circumstances leads to the conclusion that intangible forces are at work. In most cases, direct contact with the regulatory or taxing agency may be a determining factor, or there would be little justification for the army of company and industry representatives in national and state capitals.

Businessmen sense a growing involvement by government in many aspects of their affairs; there certainly have been more and more regulatory and taxing bodies. Among the areas of corporation-government contact to be considered by management are direct competition, export and import regulations and duties, special taxes on foreign investments, special tax treatments, IRS and tax court decisions and rulings, regulation of various vehicles, stock market transactions, labor relations, licensing (for example, of TV stations), regulation of advertising and packaging, and mutual help and information.

Because there are so many fronts on which industry and government meet, corporations are learning to anticipate the actions of legislators and bureaucrats. Whenever possible, business wants to discuss proposed legislation or regulation before it goes into effect. Many firms have set up special departments for government contact; others are participating in industry lobbying.

Such controversial matters as government development of electric power, protection of home industry versus unlimited imports, and taxes on foreign investments have been taken to the public through advertising, articles, and letters. Stockholders and others are asked to express themselves to legislators in behalf of the industry position.

One of the fastest-growing activities of government is control of trade, business, or professional practices. Many lines of business and most professions are licensed—some by both a state board and a city board—for revenue purposes. The securities business is tightly bound in a network of regulations that are often changed and amplified. A clean record is necessary to conduct a brokerage business, just as it is for medical practice or a bar license.

The drug business now has such strict requirements by the Food and Drug Administration that introduction of a new prescription drug may cost half a million dollars as a result of clinical demonstrations and laboratory tests. Foods are also required to demonstrate an acceptable quality and purity and to have the contents and weight clearly shown on the labels. Under a new packaging act, challenges are made to allegedly deceptive packages.

Practically all labor contract negotiations are subject to government control. A corporation's labor relations may be a flaw in its image: If it is constantly at odds with the unions, it is subject to shutdowns and strikes and consequent financial losses. There may be little that a company can do to prevent attacks by labor; yet there are firms with almost unblemished records, some of which are without union contracts.

One developing phase of the image problem should receive special consideration, namely, the company's record and reputation vis-à-vis fair employment practices laws. Both federal and state agencies are seeking to improve the employment situation for members of minority races and other hard-core unemployed, and they have used threats of contract cancellations and other penalties.

Advertising is under jurisdiction of the Federal Trade Commission and is, therefore, one more aspect of the image program that is always under certain controls.

Not all contact between business and government is adverse, by any means. Federal, state, and local bodies are tremendous customers of industry; their purchases range from the $70 billion per year of the Department of Defense to the small amount spent on paper clips for city offices. The government is a widely used source of information in some fields. Census and other statistics are the basis for market selection and quotas; figures on exports and imports guide international business; employment, cost of living, gross national product, and other items govern economic decisions on investment, expansion, and new products.

Many of the advantages of a favorable image are necessarily intangible and must to some extent be taken on faith by management. Business and industry have come to recognize that the correlation between the favorable image of a corporation and its financial success is so great that creation of such an image should be an integral part of long-range planning and consistent development.

3

The Value
of Periodic Evaluation

MOST corporations find it advisable to make a periodic evaluation of their image and their standing with customers, employees, investors, and the public. This review should consider the company itself, its progress or lack of achievement, its relative position in the industry, moves that have been made or planned to accomplish growth, existing or potential troubles, internal organization, and financial position.

Attention must also be given to the outside factors that have been changing. A position that may have been suitable only a decade ago can make a firm look like Rip Van Winkle today, so rapidly have changes been taking place in science and technology, social attitudes, new involvement of government, realignment of corporate structure—virtually every aspect of social, economic, and political life.

A statement on the effects of current conditions in the financial community is included in the following excerpt from a report of Loomis-Sayles Mutual Fund:

> Today's prudent investor is aware of change. He sees the new economic and social emphasis of our government with its eroding effects on the value of the dollar. He tries to visualize the potential scope of the tremendous technological advances of the times. He sees marked growth in the 1970s from the substantial buildup in the young adult group. He appreciates the great new demands for equity investments even when he recognizes the dangers inherent in recurring extreme speculation in the marketplace.
>
> All this means that a prudent investor requires an alert, aggressive, adaptable investment approach that will *recognize change* and do something about it.

Limit the Investigation to Essentials

Established guidelines will prevent too extensive an examination, one that may go off on unnecessary tangents. They will limit discussion to the important subjects and direct early studies as well as later conclusions. It is obvious that the nature of the corporation's business will be a primary factor in selecting the objectives and channeling the research—clearly the needs of a Wall Street underwriter are not those of a retail chain; a public utility depending on rate advances has a different problem from a maker of farm machines.

One of the first requirements is to decide which audience is really of major interest. For a merchandiser, this audience could well be the general public; certainly the general public would be important to an automobile manufacturer or proprietary drug maker. For a firm without consumer products and with a limited number of customers, priority might go to the financial community or possibly to a narrow group of technical buyers. There are companies whose greatest concern is the goodwill of their communities. Public utilities need to make a favorable impression upon regulatory bodies as well as on the people they serve, and the public can be motivated to influence government agencies.

One of the most significant changes that must be considered in almost every corporation's plans is the swing to a service economy. During 1969, it was estimated that more than 40 percent of all consumer expenditures were for services. In that year, service costs equalled the total spending of 15 years earlier.

Victor R. Fuchs, vice-president of the National Bureau of Economic Research, has predicted that the proportion of workers in service jobs will continue to grow; half of all employees are in this category now. Many of the services and the jobs they provide are not affected by economic conditions as much as manufacturing jobs. It is always necessary to go to the doctor or the barber and to send the laundry out and send children to school. For this reason, the swing to a service economy makes it more difficult to control inflation.

Business and Social Problems

Another major change in the world in which a corporation operates and presents its image is the deeper involvement of industry in social and environmental factors. This will be considered in depth in the discussion of community relations; it should be a basic concern of every corporation management.

It is no longer enough for a business to be reasonably profitable, provide employment, and pay taxes. There is strong pressure on all businesses, and particularly on large corporations, to accept more responsibility for full employment, decent housing, fair administration of local justice, clean air and water, and all other factors that contribute to the good life.

This generally means that the company will become involved in both private and governmental programs, using management time and company money for the betterment of its neighbors. Most farsighted executives realize that this activity is not only philanthropic but necessary for the preservation of the economic system and for the welfare of their own companies.

Business has largely abandoned the long-accepted idea that all it need do is operate within legal and ethical bounds and continue to grow and prosper. If it was once claimed that prosperity would take care of everyone, it is recognized now that business has to take more direct action about how a company goes about its employment practices, and rehabilitation of the hard-core unemployed is one measure of its image.

Business is rapidly learning that it can't get away with paying lip service to the social community—it must produce a workable program to fit specific needs. Efforts have been made, but so far both industry and government programs have fallen short of solving the problem. Some companies have undertaken significant programs, locating plants in ghetto areas or hiring the hard-core unemployed regardless of qualifications or previous records. But until unrest, demonstrations, and riots focused attention on the needs and demands of the ghettos, most firms worked on the principle that they would hire minority members if they could qualify. Unfortunately, not many qualified, certainly not enough to change the ratio of minority unemployment.

Following Detroit's severe riots, automobile companies went into ghetto areas to set up employment offices and established training programs for inexperienced men and women. These programs were successful only to a limited extent. Many of these people were not accustomed to workday schedules; some were even unable to find the right bus to get to a factory.

One diversified manufacturer made direct appeals for trainees, only to find that jobs were often not available when people were. There was a definite backlash in at least one community. Government-sponsored training centers found difficulty placing their graduates and getting them to stay at work.

One problem has been the attitude of present employees. They vigorously oppose the hiring of inexperienced people if they assume that this affects their own job security or possibility of advancement. Unions have actively resisted inclusion of minority-group members in their apprenticeship programs. Several cities have seen confrontations between union members and unhappy job applicants, particularly in the construction industries. Some companies have given in to their employees and hired blacks or Chicanos only under government threats to cancel contracts for unfair labor practices.

Almost every company and certainly all the large corporations face problems of race relations and fair employment. Some that have been accused of being unfair have been boycotted and picketed. This is not a clear-cut situation for any company, but it definitely is one that must be handled by management and understood by industrial and public relations departments if the firm is not to lose standing and profits.

At the 1968 annual meeting of the Ford Motor Company, Henry Ford, Jr. said:

Your company and members of its management are engaged in such activities because we believe that business and industry have an obligation to serve the nation in time of crisis, whether the danger is internal or external. It is clear, moreover, that whatever seriously threatens the stability and progress of the country and its cities also threatens the growth of the economy and your company. Prudent and constructive company efforts to help overcome the urban crisis are demanded by your company's obligations as a corporate citizen, as well as by your management's duty to safeguard your investment.

The life insurance industry has undertaken a program to put tremendous sums into slum housing, while recognizing that this investment is not likely to be as profitable as others. Of this campaign, T. F. Murray, vice-president of Equitable Life, has said, "We must conclude that industry and business have a responsibility above and beyond strictly economic concern (although this alone may be compelling) to solve the problems of the city core areas."

The extent of attacks on a corporate image is seen in the protests and riots against Dow Chemical Company for its part in manufacturing napalm for the Department of Defense. Dow's recruiters were mobbed on some campuses, but according to reports, there was a reaction in 1969, and more than normal numbers of graduates are now applying for appointments. Retailers find that some housewives will not buy Dow products that they formerly used. In its defense, the company has explained that napalm is no more than 1 or 2 percent of its total business, and that it was asked by the government to help with the war effort.

Employment ratios and the lack of opportunities for advancement available to minority groups are at the heart of the problems facing industry. National and state fair employment departments have challenged the records of a number of corporations, particularly where the ratio is openly apparent, as it is in banks and retail stores. There have been threatened boycotts against firms that were considered unfair by protestors. A long boycott against California table grapes was partially due to race relations and has been widely publicized in this country and abroad.

On the other hand, completely new standards for employment have been adopted by a number of firms that are making opportunities for former convicts, untrained dropouts, and handicapped persons. Between these extremes, most managements seek to keep peace in their communities without too much loss of working efficiency. Under present conditions, that can be one of the major concerns when corporate plans and images are evaluated.

The new obligations of the corporation do not stop at the door of the employment office. Business is being called on to help solve educational problems, provide better systems of health protection, and contribute to workable welfare programs. At the 1969 annual meeting of the Times Mirror Company, the principal emphasis was on social changes and the responsibility of business to work toward improvement. The *Los Angeles Times* sponsors a schedule of special events to benefit the youth of the community that results in contributions of nearly $6 million for charitable causes.

Protection of the Consumer

Increased governmental activity and legislation have made corporations increasingly aware of their responsibility to their customers. One of the controversial requirements for automobile manufacturers is a reduction in air pollution, and there are government agencies and individual crusaders pushing the manufacturers to more effective devices and better service on those installed. One house of the California legislature passed a law against the sale of internal combustion engines after 1975, which later failed to pass in the upper house, and the threat of electric or steam cars sends shivers through the automobile and petroleum industries. All these are relatively new problems that seriously affect the image, as well as the operations, of entire industries and individual corporations and that must be faced in future planning.

Racing has been publicized, off and on over the years, to build the auto makers' image. For some years, there was a general withdrawal from company-sponsored racing, the policy being a de-emphasis on power and speed. With the recent introduction of sports models by all the makers, racing is now sponsored or condoned with keen rivalry.

In a countermove, the car builders are also currently emphasizing safety, partly because of public and government pressure. Accusations have been made that safety devices are delayed because they are costly. Under direct government orders, a number of features have been added to all cars, including imports.

As a direct challenge to General Motors, the largest American corporation, an active campaign to place three representatives of the public on the GM board of directors was carried to the 1970 annual meeting. These members were to bring pressure on the company for more rapid solution of the problems of air pollution, safety, and service. Although the campaign gained only a small fraction of the stockholder votes, it was endorsed by some prestigious institutions and could be the forerunner of further action.

The Federal Transportation Department is another agency entering this field. United States tire manufacturers and foreign companies have been asked to show cause why these firms should not be penalized for apparent violation of safety requirements. It is impossible to create an image that offsets convictions, but it may be critical for a company to defend itself against *alleged* violations, and here a good reputation can be of help.

Another shadowy but vital area is the possibility of contingent liability of a manufacturer, such as occurs when an accident is said to result from a faulty car or poisoning from contaminated foods. This is one reason that auto makers have recalled hundreds of thousands of cars for parts replacement or adjustment, and the industry has adopted a policy of wide publicity for such recalls.

In addition to advertising and promotion for individual models, auto builders spend large sums on their corporate image to convince prospective customers that each of their divisions is a leader and that, as a company, they are innovative and working in the public welfare. When a new model makes a big hit, this reflects to the advantage of the entire corporation. It is reported that General Motors has spent more than $50 million to build public acceptance and approval. One advertising campaign concentrated solely on the GM symbol, without identification or description of any specific automobile, only a listing of divisions. One advertisement emphasized that GM offers 190 different models in a range for every customer. Other copy says "Keep Your Car All GM," urging that service, parts, and replacements be those of the company and its dealers.

Available Options

Food companies have a number of options in the image they present to consumers, and they must review their position to make certain that they are not being displaced. A manufacturer may elect to offer products in higher price brackets, either for a general line or in specialties, to attract an affluent but limited patronage. Another food firm may choose the other extreme and take the lead in low prices or discounts. Dependability throughout a wide line of branded products is the mark of successful large producers.

In recent years there have been an increasing number of foods that appeal to certain groups—health foods, weight reduction foods or formulas to meet diet demands, and fads. Or the special appeal may be convenient preparation or packaging to reduce kitchen time and effort, an asset that is important to the institutional market as well as busy housewives. The increased number of items available can be seen in the inventories of supermarkets, which count 7,000 to 10,000 different products or sizes on their shelves.

A broad swing in preference can damage one firm's position and advance another's. The popularity of low-calorie soft drinks built the business or improved the market position of a number of firms, only to be shaken by a government ruling against cyclamates.

The consumer pays for the products of the ethical drug companies but cannot prescribe them for himself. So the manufacturers seek to establish their image with doctors and hospitals. This is a good illustration of a specialized target; suppliers seek a reputation that will insure success for new products as well as wider use of their standard products.

Investors Are Also Influenced

As part of its posture in the financial world, a company usually seeks to interest the growing number of individual investors as well as brokers, bankers, and analysts. According to the New York Stock Exchange, there were 30.8 million stockholders in the United States at the end of 1969, more than double the number there were ten years earlier and a gain of 10 million in four years. This represents more than one-quarter of the population over 21 years old and nearly half of all households in the country.

For corporations that depend on the public to buy their products at profitable prices, public acceptance (or company image) largely determines the attitude of investors. Investors know that if the manufacturer captures a growing share of the market, profits are almost certain to be increased. However, there is always the chance that the government may disturb this fortunate environment.

Even before any legislation is enacted, the results of a government announcement can be seen. For example, in 1969 conglomerates that had been trading favorites dropped sharply in price, although it was by no means clear how they would be affected by proposed regulations.

Government officials had stated that antitrust suits would be filed against "very large" corporations to prevent them from acquiring other large firms, even ones in different lines of business. At the same time, it was announced that no action would be taken against big firms acquiring smaller firms in other industries, a process which would be expected to increase rather than diminish competition.

Congress has been considering new legislation to limit mergers on the grounds that existing statutes do not adequately protect against excessive control. The emphasis is on size and control rather than direct reduction of competition through mergers. Campaigns to regulate mergers and monopolies were also carried on by the Department of Justice, the Federal Trade Commission, the Interstate Commerce Commission, and the Treasury Department. As a result, certain mergers have been delayed or abandoned.

An interesting example of fast turnaround on the part of certain firms was their change in attitude toward the term "conglomerate." When the stock prices of these amalgamations were jumping every day, any firm with two or more products was seeking the "conglomerate" tag. By mid-1969, with quotations down as much as 50 percent, with government action threatening and earning reports disappointing, many of the conglomerate heads tried to disavow such identity. They became "diversified," "multimarket," or "acquisitions-minded." But it is unlikely that the financial community or the government will forget which are conglomerates. One or two leading corporations went against the trend, stating that they definitely were conglomerates and proud of it.

It was apparent that some managements did not have a long-range program or firm convictions about their operations and were swayed by outside circumstances and investor attitudes. This was generally the case with newer corporations, not established firms. In fact, some older industries support stronger controls on mergers and tenders.

Investors are further influenced by awards of government contracts or permits to increase operations, which are all publicly announced. Granting new routes to airlines divides millions of dollars in revenue and is thus vigorously contested. Another extended battle has been waged over railroad mergers. All the proposed mergers have faced opposition from competing lines, from communities that fear loss of service, and from some financial institutions. Awards or reductions of defense contracts affect the volume and earnings of many firms.

Because each hearing or review in the courts is publicized, awards or denials affect the corporate image. On the stock market huge segments of the economy swing in and out of favor, and while these swings may be relatively temporary, they can be substantial.

Mergers and Internal Changes

Some corporations have found themselves in an industry that is restricted in its growth and earnings or may even be declining in volume and profits. This motivates mergers, in which one firm joins another that is better situated, and holding companies by banks and railroads that permit a wider range of activities than their original charters provided.

Image revision is virtually forced on many corporations that have been formed by mergers or have grown and changed through acquisitions. These firms look nothing like the original companies, and the extent of change must be made known to customers and investors.

U.S. Industries made more acquisitions in 1968 than any other corporation—a total of 28. This company, which only a few years ago specialized in construction and industrial equipment, now deals in apparel and accessories, building materials and furnishings, and a wide range of consumer durables and services. All the divisions and products have been blanketed under the name U.S. Industries—fortunately, one that is nonspecific enough for all identities.

According to President John Billera, his firm is not interested in taking over unprofitable companies and attempting to make them successful: "Companies we buy must be profitable and growing and the management must stay on to run the business. We are not in the business of buying sick companies and trying to turn them around." What was "turned around" was the company's position when Billera succeeded to the presidency in 1965. USI had a checkered record of marginal profits and deficits. As Mr. Billera put it, "USI is the only company to prove you can do badly both with one product and with many products."

The number of products has grown steadily, and acquired products have ranged from women's garments to steel pipe. The firm has been seeking medium-priced acquisitions with pretax profits of $1 million or more and records of consistent performance. There are now more than 40 divisions and growing profits, all of which have been actively kept before the attention of the public.

Images Based on Development

The image of a company, reflecting major changes in products or services, is not necessarily the result of mergers or acquisitions. In fact, many of the largest corporations are the result of internal development and aggressive promotion. Acquisitions may appear in their growth records, but the primary reason for eminence has been product and service development.

Some pioneer companies are more active in promoting their present activities than are some of the newcomers. For example, the American Telephone & Telegraph Company, as discussed in Chapter 2, has new aspects to be presented, yet does not want to totally abandon the "Ma Bell" image that attracted more shareholders than any other corporation has. A principal objective will always be reasonable returns on investment, about which the company is jousting with government on several fronts. In the technical world and the financial community, "Ma Bell" is giving way to the "Phone Is Alive" concept, which presents the achievements of research and manufacturing divisions in space, communications, and service to the public.

Sears, Roebuck capitalized on the changes that resulted in its present image by issuing souvenir copies of the first mail-order catalog, which attracted wide attention. The company now does a great deal more business through its retail stores than by mail order, and is steadily broadening its ownership of shopping centers and its development of insurance, financing, and other services. Advertising concentrates on daily bargains but backs them up with style leadership, modern art departments, and service on major appliances.

In a heavy industry (forest products), MacMillan Bloedel realized that its identity was changing and that a more modern presentation of the company was needed. In regard to creating a corporate symbol and bringing the firm up to date, Chairman J. V. Clyne said:

> The need became more and more evident as the company expanded into new product lines and formed subsidiary companies, some of them

with names different from that of the parent company. Consistent use of the symbol will show the family relationship between them. It will be recognized wherever our name is seen or our products sold. We consider the symbol as an important step in our development as an international operation.

Impressions Are Lasting

Two firms, Brunswick Corporation and American Machine & Foundry Company, reached a peak of growth and acceptance through the success of one product line only to have their business then decline drastically. Both were popular manufacturers of bowling equipment in the early 1960s. These businesses declined, and each company rebuilt with other products, but neither has been able to replace its former boom-and-bust image.

For AMF, bowling in 1968 represented only 18 percent of income. Other sales were 35 percent industrial, 27 percent government, and 20 percent recreational. The company is a leader in cigarette machinery and is active in electrical products, process equipment, supplies for the oil industry, and parts for missiles, aircraft, and ships. Brunswick was hit equally hard by the problem of bowling alley failures, and under new management has been rebuilding with pleasure boats, medical and laboratory equipment, and other product lines.

Both firms freely admit the difficulty of reestablishing their old images but feel that both the public and the financial community are coming to recognize their *new* identities. In these two cases, revision of the corporate image became necessary but could not be achieved for several years.

Choosing a Niche and a Role

When a corporation management has examined the particular situation of its own company and that of its industry, it has just started to formulate a future image. The company's plans must be projected against the overall economy, in which two of the yardsticks are growth and change. It should be repeated that yesterday's image may now be outdated, that its objectives may need revision, and that the old programs may be as obsolete as last year's fashions.

A number of companies have been concerned about the proportion of their business devoted to defense and the investing public's subsequent reaction. Some managements have altogether avoided government contracts and production of military materials; others have tried to reduce the percentage of defense business through development and sale of commercial products and the acquisition of firms that are not heavily dependent on defense.

"Samson Trends," an analysis published by Quantum Science Corporation in September 1969, stated that an end to the Vietnam war would not reduce defense spending substantially:

> Contrary to most Washington analysts, the end of war in Vietnam will not be accompanied by a sharp cutback in defense spending. Rather, assuming a Vietnam settlement within a year or so, defense expenditures should total $75 billion in fiscal year 1972, compensating for the inflation drain and Vietnam-caused program delays.

> It is unrealistic to expect that savings, resulting from a reduction of funds allocated to Southeast Asia, will be diverted to the social sector.

Strong efforts continue in Congress to limit defense spending and make funds available for social and environmental programs in this country. The total of defense spending has been no salvation for certain large corporations, particularly aerospace industries. They have been subject to severe cutbacks, renegotiations, and failure to gain new contracts. Unemployment of aerospace engineers became a national concern in 1970. Companies that had anticipated these developments and diversified into nonmilitary industries looked extremely good in contrast to some of the giants in this field.

Defense and space are only two of the areas in which scientific and technological advances have created vast enterprises. Industry and business have been modernized by the development of computers and data processing systems. It is estimated that by 1985 at least 150,000 computers will be in use in this country, operating in thousands of applications that will include medical diagnosis, architectural design, inventory and process control, space navigation, solid-state physics, and advanced educational methods.

It is also projected that so much business will be done through data processing and the electronic transfer of funds and credit that a "credit-card society" could result. So much automatic manufacturing and marketing will increase leisure time for everyone. How each corporation will fit into such situations is certainly one consideration for the future, a future that may not be long in arriving. Evaluation of the company's image will depend on its long-range planning.

In a 1969 advertisement, The Bendix Corporation states,

> If you know what's happening in fluidics, electro-optics, numerical control, infrared sensing, oceanics, fiber-optics, pattern recognition, adaptive control, microelectronics, photogrammetry, mass spectrometry, cryogenics, holography, laser technology, gas chromatrography and meteorology, you know what's happening at Bendix.

America's New Directions

The objectives and plans of a corporation 10, 20, or 30 years ago may have been based on conditions that no longer exist. To use somewhat extreme examples, think of the categories into which we separated people a generation or two ago. There are no longer "mass" and "class" markets. The division between the buying and living habits of blue collar and white collar consumers has nearly disappeared, since their incomes are almost equivalent. This is no longer a nation in which rural and urban homes are equal in number—people have crowded into the cities and suburbs.

This country has had 20 years of almost continuous growth in personal incomes, to a point where families now enjoy the privilege of selecting luxuries—their own homes, vacation travel, stylish clothes, an assortment of foods and beverages. These options no longer belong only to one class; they are available to many people, and the percentage is growing.

According to national surveys, the expenditures for recreation and leisure climb with increased income, and projections indicate that discretionary income will grow at least 50 percent by 1975. The greatest increase is expected in families with incomes between $10,000 and $15,000 a year, a group estimated to reach 22 million by 1975.

Any company that deals in consumer products has to evaluate its image in the light of these and other changes. Before World War II, women wearing pants were seldom seen on Fifth Avenue, Michigan Boulevard, Grant Avenue, or Wilshire Boulevard. Today, nobody notices what shoppers wear even in exclusive shops. Mass merchandisers are making their appeals on fashion and wide selections rather than economy alone. Firms where management anticipated these trends have prospered:

Their new image is projected through new stores, attractive packages, colorful advertising, and the attitude of employees.

Banks are offering credit cards, reserve accounts, and quick loans to people who never thought of bank service a generation ago. Brokerage houses are holding seminars to interest investors who are reading market reports for the first time. Everybody travels, with the airlines showing the greatest increase in traffic. Credit is almost universal, and to many families the only question is whether they are able to meet the payments.

Part of the modern attitude toward spending and the use of credit is a result of such measures as profit sharing, retirement plans, and social security. There is not the same urgent need to save for old age or emergencies. Only a relatively small percentage of people remember the depression of the 1930s.

Most farmers are no longer "small businessmen." Many people who live on farms work at least part time in industry, and large-scale enterprises raise most of the food and fiber. The agricultural schools emphasize mechanical harvesters for different crops and the development of fruits and vegetables that can be mechanically harvested. They teach economics and management, as well as crop rotation and plant feeding. To work the big farms requires equipment that is larger, more automatic, and far more expensive than that of earlier days.

More and more women have been drawn into industry and service work as well as into offices and stores. Family life changes as women have more income and spend less time at home. They buy laborsaving devices and prepared foods, eat more meals in restaurants, and send out the laundry and cleaning.

New Trends in Marketing

The combination of greater disposable income and reduced working hours has created a tremendous new market, namely, leisure-time satisfaction. It is not one market as such, but a wide assortment of markets for goods and services to give people pleasure when they are not working or sleeping.

In this available time, estimated at one-third of each week, people watch television, listen to radios, records, or tapes, work in the garden, or play games. They go to concerts, movies, and the theater; take a ride or fly around the world; play golf and tennis, ride horseback, fly, bowl, hunt, and fish; attend sports events and the races; become collectors, gamble, read, or go to school. These activities can take place after work, on weekends, or during vacations; they can cost little or become a major part of the family expense. All in all, they must be seriously considered in the plans of many corporations. What the company has to offer in these new and growing markets, or what it is expected to offer, is of interest both to customers and to people considering investments.

Merchandising has changed as fast as manufacturing. National organizations are growing larger, absorbing others, and concentrating ownership. Shopping units are now centers or malls rather than neighborhood corners. Discount has been the active word. Chain stores claim savings and even give up trading stamps to prove it. Department stores set up discount departments. Banks issue credit cards good for an unlimited assortment of products and services. Credit privileges have spread to the airlines, to hotel and motel chains, car and boat rentals, communications —to a point where cash is rarely essential, except at the post office. Even churches are accepting offerings on a credit-card basis.

Whether it is immediately recognized or not, all these changes in the affairs of people can affect the business of many corporations.

A new ingredient in the image of some large corporations is their participation in construction and in ownership and development of land. At first, buildings were constructed of the materials produced by the companies themselves, creating in the public's mind an obvious association. For example, steel and aluminum firms put up skyscrapers faced with these metals. Other downtown developments have been handled by financial institutions, insurance, or industrial corporations, often to provide needed offices in crowded cities.

Land ownership often results in acquisition of raw materials such as minerals or forests. Other acquisitions come from railroad ownership of land that can be developed for industry or homes. Some corporations invest in real estate for resale, promoting agricultural and residential as well as industrial use.

Another new direction for many firms is importing or manufacturing abroad. Some importers have prospered, in some instances at the expense of domestic companies. In spite of the introduction of smaller, less expensive American cars, imports of autos climbed as high as 13 percent of total sales in mid-1969. Clothing is probably the largest item of consumer imports, as apparel and shoes from many parts of the world gain fashion approval and consequent sales. Food shipments abroad are substantially greater than imports, but there is a growing market for many specialties, from frozen and canned seafoods to olive oil and pineapple. In 1968, 71 percent of the shrimp consumed in the United States was imported.

American ownership and control of industry abroad has grown rapidly, to a point where other countries have moved to limit its expansion. Many of the new plants and distributing branches are selling their products in those nations, but others result in shipments to this country.

Thus each company will do well to make a periodic examination of its recognition and reputation, and see how its image meets the new conditions brought about by economic, social, and technological changes within the company, in its immediate industry, and in relation to broader conditions in this country and around the world.

4

Analyzing the Current Position

BECAUSE the corporate image is an intangible impression, existing in the minds of people as a subjective opinion, any analysis of a company's position can only be approximate. Nonetheless, it is essential that objectives of the image program, based on the long-range plans of the corporation, should be based on careful research. How an image is formed has been well expressed by the late Pierre Martineau, formerly of the *Chicago Tribune*, in *The Corporate Personality*.

> Most people are likely to judge a book by its cover, a product by its packaging, and a corporation by their personal knowledge of its employees, products, services, profit-and-loss statements, or of the contents and appearance of its advertising, public relations and other communications. The most important point to keep in mind when considering individual or collective attitudes is that most of these judgments are formed on the basis of symbols rather than facts. People do not react

with reality. Rather, they react with their subjective knowledge of reality.

The first step in researching the corporate posture is often the hardest; it involves, as has been discussed, a definition by management of what the company has been, what it is, and what it is expected to become. So far as possible, there should be agreement among the principal executives on these definitions; if agreement is not reached there should at least be mutual understanding. While these definitions may not be completely accurate, they become a starting point and will have a bearing on everything done by the organization. The next step is evaluation, followed by outside research.

Self-examination may start with a review of the company's history—where and when progress was made or mistakes committed. There will be a careful look at all the symbols of identity, the visual presentation of the corporation, to see whether they accurately represent the company. This will lead to a consideration of what should be retained and what discarded, the ways the corporation has changed and what it currently does, how it has been presented through advertising, reports, and other communications, and how it stands in relation to other corporations. Perhaps most important of all is an understanding of the company's business philosophy—the plans and dreams of its management.

The Importance of Outside Research

Self-analysis by the firm's executives is not often completely objective, and an image program should not be based solely on internal judgment. What is needed is a careful check of the way in which certain people regard the corporation. These people are not going to express themselves fully or honestly to representatives of management.

Research studies in leading universities show that the internal evaluation of a company's image is seldom the same as that of outsiders. In one study, a panel of senior executives, government officials, and heads of business schools was asked to rate 100 of the largest corporations on one point—was the firm considered innovative? There was a high correlation among members of the panel, but when managements of the rated companies were asked their opinions, most of the firms claimed an image of innovation and progressive management that had not been awarded them by the outside judges.

A reasonably accurate picture of a company can be obtained from one of the research organizations that specialize in such studies. Then it is important that the research findings be carefully considered by management. This is done not to question the methods or the answers, but to project possible changes to improve the image. It is important to remember that any image must reflect what the company *really* is, and no image program can project for long any different picture. Research will not reveal all the characteristics of the corporation, but it will often open management's eyes not only to what outsiders believe but to what the company really is.

If the research is to be a broad study that precedes a major change in the corporate image or identity, it will usually analyze the existing strengths and weaknesses of the company. It will seek to learn which characteristics are well known and regarded and which policies or practices create an unfavorable response. This will become management's guide in its selection of what to retain and what to change.

The experience of DiGiorgio Corporation shows that management may not realize how little outsiders know about changes in an established corporation. This firm made a survey of financial executives in a number of cities to find out what they knew about DiGiorgio and, as President Robert DiGiorgio told the Los Angeles Society of Financial Analysts in June 1969, the amount of misinformation was shocking.

Even in San Francisco, where the company has had headquarters for many years, most financial men thought DiGiorgio was essentially a farming organization. In fact, most of the agricultural property has been sold, and farming is only 3 percent of the total revenue. Only one in ten of the financial executives interviewed knew of DiGiorgio's activity in forest products, which account for 30 percent of net income, and only 4 percent recognized the firm's entry into pharmaceuticals. The corporation's business is ten times that of the family farm-based activities of ten years ago.

Easier to Assess Identity

The corporate identity is represented by symbols, trademarks, logotypes, packages, signs, and other physical properties, so it can be assessed more accurately than the intangible image. It is not difficult to establish ,

As expressed in stock quotations, the public places a higher value on companies that are considered innovative. This analysis, from the Sloan School of Management, M.I.T., shows a consistent market trend of two stock groups. (*Source: Moody's Handbook of Common Stocks, Fourth Quarter, 1968*)

Average Percent Change In Market Price – 1963-1967

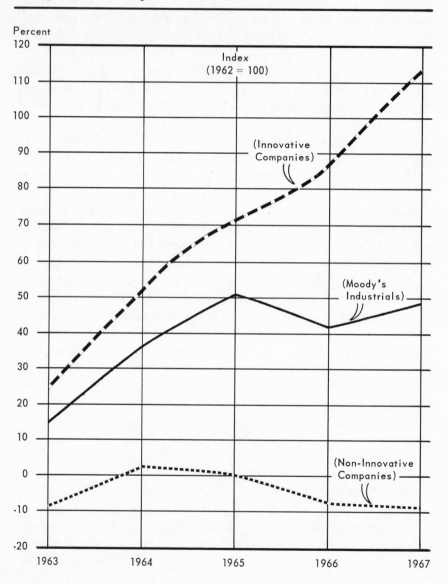

what percentage of people recognize the firm's identifying emblems or to check how many have recognized a new look at any stage in the program. This survey of recognition is helpful, especially in connection with the introduction of a new name or major mark, but this is by no means a complete analysis of the corporate image.

For companies that are about to introduce a new identity, another phase of research is a general consideration of names, symbols, trademarks, and other physical representations. This study should consider current trends and possible conflicts or confusion, making certain that the new name or symbol will not limit the firm at some future date. The psychological appeals of various emblems can be important. How well symbols can be applied in all means of communication must be considered—how they will look in advertising, on stationery, vehicles, plant signs, and other places.

Research organizations, design groups, and corporate executives tend to agree that the evaluation of a company symbol is an internal function, and that the only value of outside research on such identification is to check on its recognizability. Outsiders cannot separate their opinions of symbols from their image of the whole corporation.

Computers can devise every possible name or identification, and at least a few corporations have made a selection on that basis. Others suggest that the computer offerings should be weighed against personal judgment to avoid adoption of an identity that could later become dated or even freakish.

Bank of America made its first survey of its image in 1954 among 2,000 businessmen throughout the United States. This was a period during which the bank was expanding its activities in this country and abroad. The findings of the 1954 study have been used as guidelines for further studies. It has been found that a three-year period between surveys is optimum for the purpose.

Special studies have been made from time to time in specific groups to examine problems and possibilities in those areas. In 1969, Bank of America management felt that its image among California customers should be reviewed, and so a survey was made in all parts of the state by an outside organization. In addition to general questions on the image of the bank, comparisons were made with "an ideal bank" and with other institutions in California, rating such points as size, stability, efficiency, progressiveness, and friendliness. Management was surprised at some of the findings and decided that action should be promptly taken to correct what it regarded as misunderstandings. Kenneth Larkin, senior vice-president in charge of marketing, stated:

> They thought we were very large, very stable, very international, but perhaps so big we had become somewhat impersonal and somewhat inefficient. . . . analysis of our operations with competing banks reassured us of our internal efficiency, but it became evident that we would have to work harder to persuade customers to view us as efficient and concerned with their needs.

In coordination with Walter Landor & Associates, San Francisco designers and consultants, a six-point program was outlined:

1. Corporate self-assessment
2. Research and evaluation
3. Statement of overall objectives and strategy
4. Development of the identification system
5. Image research
6. Implementation and continuity

Introduction of a new trademark and logotype has been a major part of the program. The bank had previously used a medallion symbol featuring the U.S.S. *Portsmouth* and a number of other marks without uniformity. The new symbol is a combination of the letters *B* and *A* in contemporary design. Employees in all branches were promptly informed of the new symbol, its significance, and its appropriate use by means of a sound-slide film. Exact standards for type faces and sizes were later set forth in a communications manual. The identity program coincided with the opening of a new headquarters building for Bank of America and the showing of a motion picture about the new structure.

Since 1959 Opinion Research Corporation has been conducting comprehensive surveys on the reputation of industry in general and of specific corporations. These studies describe the public attitude toward big business and certain industries and the relative position of participating companies. The findings on general questions are made generally available; reports on individual firms are confidential.

ORC points out that as budgets for corporate communications and information programs have grown, companies have become more aware of the need to measure the effects of these programs. Research provides feedback and control for the campaigns just as it does for other operations.

BANK OF AMERICA

Bank of America
NATIONAL TRUST AND SAVINGS ASSOCIATION
MEMBER FEDERAL DEPOSIT INSURANCE CORPORATION

An ORC study for a corporation may be simply a check for recognition of the name and products, a survey of competitive positions, a depth study of all aspects of corporate reputation, or a detailed investigation of specific problems. Returns can be classified according to groups of respondents by such variables as sex, age, income, occupation, stock ownership, race, and location. The results of promotion campaigns can be checked.

Not every change in an image is advantageous, as shown by the loss of recognition that followed one name change. Although the new identity was heavily advertised, only 51 percent of the respondents recognized it, as contrasted to the 83 percent that knew the old name.

Opinion Research Corporation conducted a survey of adult men and women to classify leading trademarks. The symbols were rated as "modern or abstract," "pictorial or representational," "traditional or heraldic." Conclusions drawn from the study were:

> Traditional trademarks tend to create the impression of a fine, old company in the consumer field—stable and conservative rather than exciting. By comparison, trademarks that depart from the familiar and utilize abstract forms suggest excitement and youth, a forward-looking, scientifically oriented company that stresses progressive action.

The merits of a name change and the possibilities of avoiding problems through pretesting the suggested new identities have been demonstrated for many companies. Among the elements of an effective corporate name are ease of recall and pronunciation, idea association, product association, and acceptability.

Preconceived management opinions can be proved erroneous by outside researchers. A name or symbol that is considered desirable in the board room may not be favored by customers or investors. Companies that would never consider offering a new product without careful market testing have been known, to their sorrow, to present a new identity with no previous testing of public response.

Name requirements are more stringent for corporations that do business around the world. The new name must not only be appropriate in the United States; it must be easy to use and remember and inoffensive wherever the company goes. One proposed name seemed innocuous, but in one Mideast nation this word translated as "horse manure." Other problems have arisen with names that are difficult or even impossible to pronounce in other languages because they use letters that are not found in other alphabets or combinations that do not fit foreign tongues.

Depth Studies

A full review of the corporation's image would duplicate many of the studies it makes when checking a possible acquisition. This study should only be carried far enough to establish a consensus on each point in question. In other words, when a pattern of response has been established and can only be repeated, there need be no more interviews on that point. Such a study can usually be done only by personal contact; enough confidence on the part of respondents must be gained to obtain true and complete answers. This means that a qualified questioner must obtain introductions to or otherwise establish contacts with equally qualified respondents.

An investment counsel reports on the steps taken in an analysis of a family-owned company in which there were no guidelines of security quotations or other published information. The methods could be used for the examination of any firm by an outside organization.

By asking questions about several companies in the same field, it is possible to get statements on their relative reputations without disclosing the identity of the target firm. In the reported study, the seven groups questioned were as follows:

1. *Research and development organizations,* both independent ones and those operated by competing firms, so as to evaluate the relative scientific standing and the importance of R&D in each firm.

2. *Customers,* in order to judge the merits of products and service and to establish the length of time each had been served as well as their reasons for changing suppliers.

3. *Editors and publishers of business periodicals* in the field under examination, for their opinions on the standing of various companies.

4. *Banks and other financial institutions,* for their views on the profitability and growth of the various companies as well as their opinions of the management ability in each.

5. *Distributors and dealers* in the business, to determine the consumer acceptance of various products, deliveries, and other services of the competing companies.

6. *Competitors,* for impressions about the standing of others.

7. *Major suppliers,* for information on growth, new products, and other indications of progress.

This study produced an accurate evaluation of the company and its image and, as a by-product, revealed a flaw in technical service that was of growing importance to customers but not recognized by management. Evidence of unexpected new competition was also indicated.

Existing circumstances or possible changes will often influence the direction of research; therefore, the investigation will answer important questions. There may be a pending merger or acquisition that will change the corporate identity. Entry into new markets or introduction of new products may be important in the company's future. Often there are financial considerations, and it is necessary to forecast the actions of bankers, brokers, and investors.

Research Meets Specific Problems

Company A proposes to bring out a new line of products in a highly technical field. The project will require substantial financing and can be a major factor in the firm's growth. So it becomes important to know whether Company A is regarded as capable of such development, whether it is considered able in scientific research and technical development, and whether its management can handle a new and diversified venture.

These questions are considered within the organization, of course, but it is not always enough to make a self-appraisal. Whose opinion is to be sought and what questions are to be asked? Should the survey include present customers, prospective buyers, competitors, bankers, investors, research directors? The survey must be done carefully or the results can be misleading.

As such a study is usually delegated to a research or fact-finding agency, Company A will seek assistance from an organization that is familiar with its particular field. It will try to get counsel that is dependable and aware of the confidential nature of the assignment. Some of the methods of selecting outside consultants will be considered in Chapter 10.

Should the inquiry be simple—an expression of opinion as in a political poll—or be based on depth interviews to determine reasons for the response? The approach should be worked out with the researchers. Usually, the more involved questionnaires call for a smaller number of interviews than does a simple opinion poll.

Company B wants more stockholders in order to qualify for listing on one of the major exchanges. So it needs to know whether investors are disposed to buy its stock. Do they know about the company? What do they think it makes, and how big do they think it is? Are they impressed with its record, and do they believe it will continue to grow rapidly? If not, why not?

The research organization does not just ask a number of people these direct questions as a rule. It will probably talk with investors about a number of companies. The technique may be to discuss one segment of an industry to get opinions on the future of various firms. As a result of experience, the research organization knows how to build a list for either direct or mail contacts that fits the desired pattern. The questionnaire is nearly always a result of cooperation between the client and research counsel.

The first survey for a corporation may be quite general, to set bench marks on the firm's position. Later studies may be more specific. It is important that research be continued if progress or lack of progress is to be indicated.

Any opinion poll has problems and limitations, as is shown by the variances among political polls. If the corporation's survey reports a position that is not accurate, the entire public relations program can start off in a wrong direction. False objectives will be set and incorrect methods chosen. It is nearly always best to use a competent outside organization rather than the company staff, unless it is unusually qualified.

Research organizations use the principle of random sampling for successful opinion studies. Depending on the number of logical respondents and the extent of the interview or questionnaire, accurate results are obtained from a small percentage of the total field. Political pollsters in 1968 took samples that averaged 1,500 people. One of the leading surveys of consumer planning that has had an outstanding record for many years involves interviews with 2,000 persons. This is a depth study, with an hour or more spent on each contact. It produces information on which government and industry have come to rely.

Once the respondents are selected for this national survey, interviewers are not permitted to make any changes in the list. If they fail to find a designated respondent at home, they must return until the contact is made. Most political polls permit interviewers to substitute the family next door or at a certain address in the specified block.

The questionnaire should be prepared by experienced survey people and must be based on the information the client is looking for. There should be no leading questions—only objective ones. It is equally necessary that the respondents fully answer the questions. The questionnaire may or may not be filled out during the interview; in some cases, it is preferable to make notes (tape recorders are increasingly used) and prepare the forms later.

Research through direct contact is expensive, and some companies have been successful in the use of mailed questionnaires. In most cases, the mailing includes a note of explanation, the questions, and perhaps a small gift. Pens or pencils are effective gifts as the questionnaire conveniently provides the first chance to use them.

Most surveyors are not content with one mailing. If they receive 40 percent returns from the first, they send a second questionnaire to the other 60 percent. This may be repeated two or three times, until a representative sample has answered. People who are too busy to answer the first questionnaire are likely to have different responses from the first group of respondents.

Or, to employ another method, the questionnaire can be treated as an industry study, with the results to be shared later with the respondents. Where there are questions of real interest to certain people, this method has been successful and relatively inexpensive. One of the highest returns on record came from a questionnaire in which the sender claimed the answers would be the basis of a university thesis.

For some surveys, the stockholders can provide an excellent sample. They are usually simply asked to help the company in which they have an interest. Opinions on products and proposed changes are sometimes solicited, providing an indirect opportunity to report any dissatisfaction with products or services.

Some companies set up a department to handle customer relations and check these contacts carefully for indications of favorable or unfavorable opinions. There is a good deal to be learned from the contact of salespeople with customers, but the reports should be carefully evaluated.

Survey methods used should have the full support of the entire management. Research that is regarded with suspicion is worse than none at all, and it can be trusted only if handled by competent people and backed by the client organization.

Another special circumstance in which management should seek an accurate evaluation of the company's image is when the firm may be up for sale or merger. Unless there has been a careful analysis of the company's position and a study of the possible buyers, the best possible deal may not be made. As the sale or merger of a firm is irrevocable, this is one of the most important decisions that management will ever make.

In spite of the growing number of amalgamations, few companies ever openly admit that they are on the market. In 1969 the National Industrial Conference Board reported that out of 96 corporations of moderate size, 46 expressed firm intentions of remaining independent and only 4 were actively seeking to sell or merge.

The importance of the corporate image becomes highly evident whenever a sale or merger is considered. Not only financial statistics are considered by prospective buyers. More corporations are using outside counsel or bank assistance in planning for a sale or merger. This permits an evaluation of the company without first disclosing its identity. Careful preparation should be made to demonstrate the advantages of the corporation to possible buyers and show them the favorable results of a proposed union.

How a Design and Identity Consultant Works

How a design and identity consultant approaches research is illustrated by this summary of what Lippincott & Margulies did for RCA.

The work began with a detailed analysis of what RCA's objectives seemed to be and what people—in government, the financial community, shareholders, customers, employees, prospective employees—think of the company, and, finally, what it is actually saying to them. In order to accomplish this, the L&M project team conferred at length with RCA executives and studied all relevant operating procedures. The team examined at first hand the facilities—from TV plants in Indianapolis and recording studios in Rome to microwave labs in Montreal and launching pads at Cape Kennedy. Volumes of corporate publications and executive speeches and hundreds of commercials and ads were evaluated and thousands of products and packages, sales brochures, and signs were assessed. Lippincott & Margulies's report states:

> A new approach was needed to reflect the scope and dynamism of a major corporation involved with every principal aspect of information technology, from broadcasting and publishing to computers and educational systems.

Unmistakably, the outward face which RCA showed to its publics did not measure up to its inner reality. Moreover, the communicative structure for accomplishing past and present objectives could never successfully help to carry out new objectives.

Reactions to selected media indicate that opinion leaders are influenced by publications and that their own acceptance of ideas will create changes in public opinion. Campaigns that are directed toward opinion leaders have been a favored communications method and one that can be used to advantage in presenting a corporate image.

From time to time, advertising and public relations have borrowed ideas from psychology. Several years ago the idea was advanced and widely discussed that people could be influenced without their knowledge. These so-called *subliminal messages* were to accompany advertising or political appeals on television and were supposed to register an impression without the conscious awareness of the viewer. Some proponents claimed impressive results.

Another technique that burst on the communications world only to fade rapidly was *motivational research*. Through MR, advertisers could determine in advance what appeals would influence potential customers and then use these appeals to improve their campaigns. The idea is valid, but its deployment called for depth interviews by professional psychiatrists at an unjustifiable cost in time and money.

There is reason to believe that developments in the behavioral sciences can be helpful in fashioning corporate images and that some new concepts will have business applications.

Executives Evaluate Research

When reports from external and internal research are received, it is management's responsibility to review and analyze the corporate image as shown. This becomes the basis for setting objectives of a new program, answering problems that may have appeared, and capitalizing on apparent advantages and opportunities.

It should again be emphasized that a rapid change in the corporate image is difficult to accomplish. Even a selected audience will be slow to respond. The new image that seems so important to management is, after all, not usually of great interest to outsiders.

Among corporations where management has changed and new plans have been projected, a reversal of public opinion has taken longer than expected, according to recent studies. Several years usually pass before a corporation can gain its desired image, which must be based on performance rather than promises. Certainly the announcement of changes and their continued promotion have an effect, but it is often more gradual than expected.

The rapidity with which a new image can be registered is in direct proportion to the specific interest of the respondents. While it may take years to reverse the opinion of the general public, a concentrated campaign to security analysts can be quickly effective if new information affects the investor's interests and attitude.

Research studies unanimously agree that the corporate image is a reflection of top management attitudes. The inspiration and motivation for a favorable image comes from a dynamic top executive or an equally effective management committee. This is repeatedly confirmed by investment bankers and analysts when they label companies as "progressive" and "prosperous."

When there is a complete change pending after an amalgamation or the entry into another industry, management must also consider how this new identity is to be presented. As described in Chapter 1, the possibilities range all the way from a completely new identity to a shortened name.

Another phase of research will be identification of the opinion leaders to whom the changed image will be directed. Depending on the company's needs and plans, these can be government officials and representatives, financial managers, community leaders, employees, unions, educators, and other specific audiences. If there is a new trademark, it should receive general publicity.

According to "The Language of Corporate Trademarks and Symbols" by Opinion Research Corporation,

> The company trademark, repeated millions of times each year, has vast potential for communicating what the company stands for.

> Research on 121 trademarks reveals important principles in the language of symbols and shows how the trademark can be integrated with overall communications strategy.

The degree of accuracy needed in the research should be considered. If a general consensus will be a satisfactory guide toward objectives, research need not be as detailed as it would if exact percentages were sought.

Any interviewing method or questionnaire should be well tested in advance of general use and results of the tests thoroughly checked. Field work, either by employees or outside interviewers, should be checked and carefully interpreted.

5

Setting Objectives
for the Image Program

SOME of the most important choices for management are the objectives
of the corporate image campaign. These choices, of course, involve the
long-range planning for the company's future, the establishment of expansion and profit targets, and the means by which these targets can be
reached. No matter how impressive the firm's achievements are, they
must be properly presented if the public is to acknowledge them. Thus
planning for a favorable image is an integral part of policy decisions.

The accuracy with which objectives for the corporate image can be
set will depend on the results of research into the firm's existing position
and potential change. This research, as outlined in Chapter 4, can con-
structively guide all the company's plans or it can sadly mislead. It must
be assumed that management has carefully checked the research methods
and results and is prepared to accept them.

As part of the overall planning for the corporation, the image program will usually have several long- or short-range objectives. Priorities should be established for each, depending on its importance and the timing involved. For most companies, an image program is part of broad planning for greater sales and profits. This is the fundamental objective of management, and all its activities will be programmed to that end. There will be other concerns for most corporations, but they will usually be subsidiary to the major target.

Pragmatic Limitations

When the objectives of an image program are considered, the means by which they can be gained should be kept in mind. It makes little sense to set up a campaign that cannot be supported by action. There will always be some limits to what can reasonably be accomplished, and it is better to exceed what is promised than to fall short.

Since the corporate image is an intangible concept, the possible impact on various audiences can be predicted only in part. This does not mean that objectives cannot be firmly and specifically outlined; it does follow that they may not be fully attained. To some extent this is a matter of communications—a subject that is receiving a great deal of attention but is still far from exact. Some corporations have set up departments for the study and improvement of their communications, both internal and external; others are using the services of experienced outside agencies.

It should be remembered that it usually takes more time than is expected to change the public's ideas of a corporation. The general public, excepting shareholders and those doing business with the company, have no particular interest in the corporation's changes, its accomplishments, or its image. The public has no established interest in a company as it does in products, so the best that can be anticipated is a gradual elevation of opinion. This, again, depends on the progress of the firm. If it has an outstanding record of development, undergoes substantial changes, or is supported by effective advertising and promotion, recognition of its changing image can be faster.

Limitations may exist within the corporation. There may not be enough money to make rapid changes and promote growth. Problems of management or product development slow down many a brave program.

These limitations must be considered when management sets objectives, both for the corporation and its image.

Delays in substantial public reaction are confirmed by behavioral scientists, who claim that there are definite limits to what can be accomplished by mass communications. Their findings indicate that, in many instances, advertising, publicity, speeches, and other appeals do little to change existing opinions. They report that total conversions to a different point of view are rare, although minor changes in opinion may be provoked.

If it is agreed that these studies are applicable to changes in a corporate image, it becomes more important than ever to establish a satisfactory image from the start. Most people have an established opinion of the firms they know; they consider them progressive or old-fashioned, successful or failing, agreeable or difficult in business relations, open to change or closed-minded, good or bad neighbors in the community.

As a result of developments over a long period, a corporation may no longer fit its former identity. This, at least, gives management an opportunity to study the existing position and to chart a course toward desired objectives without pressure.

Another condition prevails when the company is a partner in a merger, has been through a series of negotiations and tenders, or has faced a financial crisis or other emergency. Then the immediate objective of the image program is an announcement or an explanation to try to make the changes appear as favorable as possible. Such a situation should have been anticipated some time before the announcement is necessary, and management should set a policy for the program and make certain that the people charged with its execution are aware of its problems and possibilities.

Whether emergencies threaten or not, company policy should be set in advance. This should cover the handling of government inquiries and investigations, plant or personnel catastrophes, the discovery of loss of important resources, major changes in earnings forecasts, financial reverses, challenges to management, and other problems that may be faced.

As one of the larger conglomerates, Ling-Temco-Vought was the first attacked under a federal policy of limiting the scope of these diversified corporations. The specific suit was to prevent LTV from acquiring Jones & Laughlin Steel Company through a merger to which both corporations had agreed.

With its annual report, Ling-Temco-Vought sent to all shareholders an eight-page letter, charging that an anticonglomerate campaign had been waged by certain officials and asking shareholders to write to legislators. A 15-point rebuttal was included. The letter mentioned Ford, RCA, General Electric, and General Motors as multi-industry enterprises that have done "an outstanding job of serving the public." Under severe financial as well as regulatory pressure, LTV in 1970 announced the sale of several divisions and subsidiaries and the reorganization of its financial structure. James Ling, founder and long-time president, was replaced as chief executive.

How Should a Company Choose Policy?

The objectives of a retail organization or of a manufacturer selling consumer products through its own dealer organization can be more readily defined than those of a newly formed conglomerate that has absorbed a dozen diverse enterprises. The retailer may be a promotional firm that stresses price appeals, it may be primarily a service organization, or a firm that trades on prestige.

The images of Tiffany, Dunhill, and Neiman-Marcus have been built successfully over a long period of time. Their identities are deliberately designed to attract certain customers. The objective of such stores is the preservation of this appeal, of this image, which is the result of a consistent tone in decor, advertising, and publicity as well as in the type of merchandise offered. Some of the devices used to sustain these images may seem extreme but are usually in keeping with what the public expects from such stores.

The service organizations—banks, brokers, transportation companies, laundry and cleaning firms, builders, maintenance organizations, hospitals, hotels, and hundreds of others—will be primarily concerned with customers in the mass. Some will be regular patrons, but many will be new. Manufacturers of consumer goods are also looking to the general public for customers.

An industrial corporation has customers, too, but they may be limited in number and confined to a narrow segment of business or government. It may be more important for the corporation to attract the interest and support of investors and to protect its position with principal customers than to woo the general public.

Financial institutions, transportation companies, and public utilities may have problems of rates or regulations that are more important, at least at the moment, than any contacts with customers or investors. Whatever value the image has in these circumstances has usually been developed over a period of time. There are always certain situations in which a business will look to its shareholders or the general public for support.

What Shall the Corporation Represent?

The selection and rating of objectives for the image program comes down simply to the choice of what should be said and done, and to whom the appeals shall be directed. What qualities do you want to emphasize, what ready associations do you want to evoke in the public's mind? The following list includes some characteristics about which people have impressions, whether the qualities have been stressed or passively allowed to germinate. Each company must decide which of these qualities it wants to stress:

Innovative	Working to improve social conditions
Growing	Dedicated to the capitalist system
Modern	Developing capable young managers
Excellent in research	Interested in acquisitions
Favored by customers	Determined to remain independent
Profitable	Free of labor trouble
Well managed	Considered a good employer
Diversified	Sponsoring education or the arts
Market oriented	Liberal with dividends
A good neighbor	Developing international trade
Liked by suppliers	Successful in important litigation
Fair with competitors	Producing good products

To which audiences will specific appeals be directed? A priority should be set for the various targets and objectives established for each. The principal audience may be one or more of these:

Stockholders	Employees
Potential investors	Prospective employees
Sources of financing	Government agencies
Customers	Legislators
Prospective customers	Possible acquisitions
Suppliers	Potential buyers
Competitors	The general public
Plant communities	

Most corporations launching new image programs seek to look innovative, to show diversification, active research and development, entry into new markets, accommodation to social and economic changes. At the same time, the company must be operated within certain pragmatic bounds. The balance of rapid development and stability must be maintained in every corporation. Management seeks to keep them in balance and still sustain a progressive image. The problem is stated by Donald A. Schon.

> The society of a corporation attempts to maintain a stable state. This effort is not inertia but conservative dynamism. The various forms of corporate resistance to change which reflect themselves as obstacles to technological innovation are processes of conservation essential to the survival of any social or biological organism. It is nonsense to require companies to throw off this old-fashioned habit. But it is the crisis of modern industrial corporations that they are also required to undertake technical change destructive to their stable states in order to survive. It is this paradox which makes them vulnerable, accounts for their ambivalence to innovation, and forces them to adopt new forms and styles of change.*

University studies have shown that the spirit of innovation and appreciation of resourcefulness greatly affect the attitude and performance of employees. In some firms, there is a feeling of complete freedom and ability to communicate in any necessary direction. In others, managers and supervisors report that they do not know what is going on in other parts of the company and are not encouraged to inquire. There is evidence that communications become more difficult as firms grow in size and, particularly, as they diversify.

Employee acceptance of an image of freedom and progress depends almost entirely on the employee's understanding of the attitude and policies of management. If it is generally understood that new ideas are to be tried out, this will become the practice of workers and supervisors. If employees sense that the penalty for failure of a new idea will be severe, there is little chance that effective changes will be attempted. The atmosphere of challenge and opportunity that pervades some organizations also comes through to men and women who consider working for that corporation.

* *Technology and Change* (New York: A Seymour Lawrence Book/Delacorte Press, 1967).

New Names, New Images

As has been noted, thousands of corporations have been sold, merged, or gone out of business in the past few years. In many of these transactions, a new corporate name was created, and it is reasonable to expect that new names and symbols will be announced by even more firms in the next few years.

Not all the new names are the result of amalgamations. More than one corporation has created a new identity that better represents the firm's present business. A few corporations have simply dropped a name that was no longer in favor and introduced a new company with a new image.

The selection of a name can be one of the most significant decisions in the creation of the corporate image. If the new name is accompanied by new trademarks, the choices are even more important. Not all the christenings can be put into appropriate pigeonholes, but most of the new names and symbols are either entirely new, simplifications of existing names, combinations of two or more names, initials, modernizations, or names of products or individuals.

Most of the new trademarks and emblems introduced in recent years have been contemporary in design, although not necessarily abstract. Most firms seeking a new corporate image want to be identified with the present generation, to be considered scientific, and to appeal to youth. It is equally reasonable that certain corporations, particularly financial institutions, public utilities, and firms with a long record of identification, have retained their existing symbols or made only minor changes in traditional emblems.

Where changes, even radical ones, have been made, reports show that they are generally received with approval by customers, dealers, and stockholders and that there is little need to fear loss of identity or established relationships. This has been found true of packages and labels as well. Most firms that hesitated to change long-established labels but finally did so report only a temporary, small drop in sales.

There are exceptions—in some instances, radical packaging changes proved disastrous. Leslie Salt Company made extensive changes in package design and color; these changes were followed by an abrupt loss in its share of market. In contrast, Morton Salt Company made a number of changes in its package design between 1908 and 1968 but retained the

Morton Salt's image has kept pace with changes in design for over 50 years without losing its fundamental identification.

basic illustration, a girl with an umbrella and the slogan, "When it rains, it pours." Today's package shows a girl in contemporary clothes.

What does the corporation expect of a new name or symbol? It expects quick, easy identification and a minimum of confusion with other names or symbols. It expects the name and symbol to represent the character of the company, whether it is progressive or conservative, technical or nontechnical, national or international.

An entirely new name has been the answer for a number of amalgamations that might otherwise have inherited cumbersome or obsolete images. In recent years established companies have changed their names to shorter, more appropriate words—Amsted, Ametek, Armco, Avco, and on through the alphabet to UniRoyal and Xerox.

In one of the more extreme examples, Montgomery Ward and Container Corporation were united under Marcor, a name launched with an extensive advertising and promotion campaign. In addition to linking parts of the two names, Marcor is identified as a "marketing corporation."

More and more venerable institutions have been bringing their names and images up to date as a result of substantial changes in the corporation activities. American Tobacco has become American Brands, Inc., announcing that "American Tobacco is a great name. But it tells only part of the story." The change followed entry of the firm into the food industry (Sunshine Biscuits and Duffy-Mott) and the beverage field (James B. Beam). The added products represent about a quarter of the total business.

Controversy over the effects of cigarette smoking has dimmed the image of the tobacco companies, which for generations were considered sound and conservative investments. All the major companies are diversifying, both to add growth possibilities and to brighten their reputations. However, U.S. Tobacco, although it acquired nut and candy companies ten years ago, has made no change in its name.

When R. J. Reynolds, Inc. announced plans for its new name, this question was asked by a stockholder: "O.K. You're taking tobacco out of our name. Aren't you just playing with words?" He received this answer:

> If our nontobacco business were small business, the answer to your question would be yes. But now 14 percent of our sales are in nontobacco products. That's the foods, beverages, aluminum, packaging, and corn refining products part of our business. The part that has had a compound growth rate of 42 percent over the past five years.

One of the strong trends has been toward the adoption of initials as the corporate name or the one by which it is advertised, listed on stock exchanges, and generally known. IBM has made its trademark and identity known all over the world since the present form was adopted. Other changes for large firms were FMC for Food Machinery & Chemical Corp., SCM for Smith-Corona-Marchant, 3-M for Minnesota Mining & Manufacturing.

The RCA symbol of circled initials and a lightning bolt was one of the earliest and best known in the business world. This symbol was adopted when the company was primarily in the field of international wireless communications. By the time it was 50 years old, this segment of the business represented only 2 percent of the total, and RCA had 12,000 different products ranging from color television to advanced computers.

When a decision was made to bring the company identification up to date, RCA authorized research and design departments to suggest an appropriate change. Studies were made of other image programs, and careful analysis was made of the future directions of RCA. A complete change in the corporate image was recommended.

The name was obviously an anacronism, as the business was no longer limited either to radio or to America, but management wanted to retain the goodwill developed through use of the firm's initials as identification. Therefore these initials—the name and image of the corporation —were retained. Before the final design to modernize was adopted, thousands of drawings were checked and compared and the selections tested on products, properties, and printed materials.

A firm decision was made to concentrate primarily on the new identification at the cost of downgrading such famous marks as "Victor" and "Red Seal." Standards were set for all identification of products, plants, offices, and materials with the help of design consultants. Finally, the new look was announced in all RCA advertising and publicity.

A brief account of the changes that took place in International Telephone & Telegraph Corporation was given in Chapter 1, but a parallel can be drawn to RCA. Like RCA, which had changed so that it was no longer predominantly American or involved in radio, ITT was no longer predominantly in telegraph or telephone—or international for that matter. The symbol of a modern ITT was adopted to link many diversified industries, and one advertisement pointed out that more than half its earnings are derived from domestic divisions. ITT appears on plants, offices, and products in many different industries, from advanced electronics for spacecraft and computer programming to car rentals, from consumer loans to raw materials. So far as possible, each industry utilizes the parent corporation's identity.

Such vital changes as these are obviously initiated and supported by top management, because they affect not only identification but the entire program of long-range planning.

Names Reflect Various Pressures

At least part of the united identities is retained in the names of Atlantic Richfield Company, McDonnell Douglas, Ling-Temco-Vought, and Penn-Central Railroad. This policy is more common when financial institutions merge, because in many cases it is considered desirable to retain as much as possible of the various identities.

When a new name or symbol is to be adopted, management has to deal with the question of how much to retain and how much to change. Should the new identity be instantly recognizable as the successor to the old? Where only the form is changed, as was the case with IBM and RCA, there will be no problem of identity. But if the customer is to recognize 3-M Company as Minnesota Mining & Manufacturing or Marcor as Montgomery Ward plus Container Corporation, a strong introductory and educational campaign is called for.

In contrast is the policy of the Signal Companies, which grew rapidly from a regional oil company to a combination of petroleum products, aerospace components, heavy-duty trucks, banking, steel, and insurance. Each of the divisions continues under its original identity—Mack Trucks, Garrett Corporation, Arizona Bankcorporation, and others. The advertised theme is, "We told our companies to mind their own business." Corporate identification by symbol is limited and not directly related to any division name.

Two major California banks, Wells-Fargo and American Trust, merged. They were about the same size and each had been operating for nearly a century. It was decided, after an introductory period, to retain only the name and stagecoach symbol of Wells-Fargo. Other banks have been acquired and all brought into this identity.

However, Security First National Bank of Los Angeles incorporated the name "Pacific" when it absorbed Pacific National Bank of San Francisco. The name was changed to Security Pacific National because of the relatively strong position of the acquired bank in northern California, where it was the first office of Security Bank in that area. In both bank mergers, the value of the name selected outweighed any consideration of the costs involved in the new identification, which were substantial.

An outstanding example of a name that was changed to relate more closely to well-known products is that of Del Monte Corporation. For many years the company name was California Packing Corporation, but

The historic stagecoach has been retained and featured by Wells Fargo Bank through all its changes, mergers, and expansions.

SINCE 1852

WELLS FARGO BANK

NATIONAL ASSOCIATION

most of the products were under the Del Monte brand. As the firm broadened its product line into snack foods, beverages, and other specialties, it was decided to adopt the brand as the corporate name. Not only was this a logical move, but it is probably one image program in which the costs of physical changes were not excessive.

In 1969 another long-established company changed to a name associated with products: National Dairy became Kraftco Corporation. Advertising announced, "We're more than national. We're more than dairy. So, please don't call us National Dairy any more."

An image built around a well-known person has been successfully used throughout the history of American industry. Edison, Ford, Du Pont, Borden, Procter & Gamble, Boeing, Chrysler, and many others are the names of leading corporations. Newer technical and scientific firms bear the names of their founders, such as Hewlett-Packard, Bunker-Ramo, Northrop, and Rockwell.

Rexall Drug & Chemical Industries adopted the name of the company's president and became Dart Industries, Inc. in 1969. The contract for sale of the company's Rexall stores and franchise divisions gave exclusive rights to that name to the purchaser. One of the company executives told the annual meeting, "The best time to get a name change approved is when the earnings are going great."

Names of entertainers and sports figures have been widely used in launching franchise firms, seeking investor-operators, and building acceptance for stock offerings. "Here's Johnny" identifies a 1969 restaurant enterprise in which Johnny Carson and Swanson Enterprises, Inc., were joined. Although Swanson frozen foods had been sold to Campbell Soup Company, the new organization claimed that the Swanson family's success in their earlier venture could be transferred to the new one.

Other franchise systems have been promoted with such famous names as Minnie Pearl, Mahalia Jackson, Trini Lopez, Bart Starr, Mickey Mantle, Hank Williams, Rocky Marciano, Tony Bennett, and Eddie Arcaro. A big name and an advertising campaign have been enough to launch many "instant images" in this crowded field, and newcomers point to the success of earlier pioneers. It would be too much to expect that popularity and promotion will be enough to sustain all the entries, and some managements have already felt the effects of competition and problems of expansion. Maintenance of the image will demand performance as well as promotion.

Among the earliest and best-known symbols are those of insurance companies, some of which still survive. They may not be modern but they have been around so long that they are instantly recognized. Among widely advertised identities are Prudential's Rock of Gibraltar, the umbrella of Travelers, Hartford's stag, Continental's minuteman, the SAFECO roof, and Allstate's good hands.

In selecting a name or revising a company symbol or trademark, one of the important considerations should be its use on packages, for signs, and in advertising and literature. In some programs, advance tests are made on scale models or actual properties.

Merchandising and service corporations use symbols at every opportunity—on their stores or offices, on products and packages, shopping bags, checks, sales slips, envelopes, vehicles, in advertising and direct mail. The public immediately recognizes the symbols of Sears, Safeway, A&P, and dozens of others. These emblems have been carefully selected and designed to be distinctive. They are usually the work of industrial designers, who consult closely with the corporate management.

6

Media in the Image Program

ONCE the objectives of the image program have been firmly established, the means by which they are to be achieved can be determined. Target audiences for the program will be selected, and methods of communications with these audiences set up.

In most programs, certain targets will be more important than others. If the campaign is to feature new or improved products, customers may get first attention. If better financial standing is a major objective, the financial community is the primary target. For some companies, employee relations will be the first area in which the new image must be recognized. Government relations could be a principal concern.

If the campaign is based on a new name or symbol, every possible means of identification and recognition should be considered. The program can be direct and simple when only a symbol is changed, but general approval for an intangible—an image—of a company requires more thorough treatment. What media to use and how to use them are the concerns at this point. Involved are timing, budgets, personnel, outside assistance, and most of all, the message.

The objectives will determine the priorities and the amount of time and expense to be devoted to them. The efforts of all departments must be coordinated to formulate new policies and plans for public relations, advertising, marketing, industrial relations, and sometimes for production and finance.

At this point, the importance of planning and executing a *complete* program cannot be overemphasized. If only part of a program is set up, or if the campaign is curtailed before it is completed, the results cannot be fully effective.

It is vital that management realize that time is needed to gain recognition and acceptance for a new image. Even those who are really interested in the company are too busy to notice the improved posture of a corporation unless their attention is specifically called to it. Most people have no particular interest in the announcement of a new image, and there is constant competition for their attention. It is only through repetition and the use of different media over a considerable period of time that the new image of a company can become generally recognized.

John Turner, M.D., psychiatrist and consultant to industry, emphasized another point. In a discussion of "The Corporate Id" in a management symposium presented by the University of California and Walter Landor & Associates, he stated:

> The expression of the corporate "id" is extremely hard to keep under cover, especially insofar as subordinates are concerned. It's like the children in the home who get the impact of the parental "id." You can't lie to your children about emotional things because they'll find you out every time. I don't think you can lie to the people in your organization. So many times, I've heard men of rank say: "How did they find that? We only discussed it in our board room." You can't keep secrets. You can't lie to people in your organization. . . .
>
> Changing of the corporate "id" is very painful, as it is with the individual. Please don't embark on such an effort unless your purpose is clear, unless you have willingness to discover the nature of your corporate "id," and unless your wish to change is very solid, indeed.

Specifically, the corporate image program usually includes annual and interim reports, contacts with government, publicity, institutional advertising, products and packages, signs, colors, employee publications, dealer and service-organization training materials, meetings, motion pictures, shows and conventions, special events, and industrial, political, and public service campaigns.

Complete advance organization under the direction and control of senior management is the path to a successful image program. In some corporations, a chart is prepared of every possible outlet for information, including all channels inside and outside the organization, before the first move is made toward the promotion of the new image.

A program resulting from management decision to effect a change can be planned and implemented over a period of time, but a program forced by a major change, such as a merger, must be handled more quickly. If the company is committed to a policy of acquisitions or merger and can thus anticipate the need for a change in image, preparation for such a change is an essential part of advance planning.

Uses of the Annual Report

If there is one element in the corporate image program to which management should give its most careful attention, it is the annual report. There is no doubt that this is the most direct and effective contact between the company and its present and potential stockholders. This document will be read more thoroughly than advertising or other publicity for the company, because it tells the reader how well his money has been invested. In effect, the annual report sums up the corporate image.

Before the report is assembled, financial data will be supplied by accountants and auditors, design will be in the hands of artists and production people, and the various messages will probably be written by executives or by public relations men. Management need not be concerned with all these details, but it is important that the overall concept of the annual report and, to some extent, its contents and appearance be determined by top executives.

If there has been continuous research on the corporate image, information about the reaction to the annual report should be available. If it is not, it will be necessary to make some executive decisions so that the report will answer all reasonable questions and present the company as favorably as possible.

One of the first considerations is the audience to which the annual report is directed. Primarily, of course, the report is for stockholders. But does management want it circulated to bankers, brokers, investment counselors, and others who influence investments? Is it a medium for promoting the company's securities? In firms with consumer products, will the annual report go to dealers, distributors, and possible customers? Is the report intended to influence employee relations?

Studies of shareholders' reactions indicate that their principal concern is the financial success and growth of the corporation as stated in the year's results and comparative tables or charts. Other expressed interests include new product development, market expansion, changes in the economy that can affect the business, significant social changes, forecasts for the future, labor or government problems facing the corporation, advertising plans and costs, and research expenditures and results.

Studies indicate that many shareholders read no further than the statement of earnings per share and the comparison with former years. Failure to get deeper into the report may often be due to readers' inability to understand many of the statements and tabulations. The need for simple, clear language and readily understood illustrations has been generally reported in previous years.

Depending upon the objectives, management should establish policy in regard to two aspects of the report. The first will be the financial data to be included; the second is the physical appearance—size, colors, illustrations, and other details. This second phase will be discussed in depth in Chapter 7.

Within the limits of recognized accounting practice, there can be substantial differences in the interpretation of financial statistics. Management may have the option of writing off certain costs as they are incurred or extending them over a longer period. There are a number of means by which earnings statements can be adjusted.

Will the report break down sales and earnings by divisions or by product categories? The trend is toward disclosure of all these figures. In a comment on his firm's detailed report, Chairman James E. Robinson of Indian Head, Inc. is quoted in *The Wall Street Journal* as saying, "Frankly, we don't see any great disadvantage to breaking down financial reports to show how much each division did for sales and profits." The report has a five-year summary by divisions, and Chairman Robinson adds that a principal benefit of this new reporting setup is to show at a glance how important diversification has been to Indian Head's growth and well-being.

Among other corporations that show detailed figures by divisions or groups are D. H. Baldwin Company, Transamerica, Bangor Punta, and American Brands. The last-named company's evident purpose is to show its growing participation in products other than cigarettes.

Regulatory moves have been made to require the disclosure of earnings by divisions. In 1969, the Canadian government moved to require conglomerates to report separately for each division and made other new proposals calling for stronger control of reports on insider trading, proxy solicitation, and tenders.

One controversial question was settled when the American Institute of Certified Public Accountants issued rulings that earnings per share must be included in the statements signed by the auditors, and that these statements must show the dilution of earnings that would take place through warrants and options and all convertible securities. This means that stockholders will know what the effect of conversion of preferred stocks or bonds or the purchase of stock through warrants will be on per-share earnings.

The accounting profession imposed other rules, effective as of 1970, governing treatment of acquisitions. Most such corporate acquisitions have been treated on the financial statement through the "pooling-of-interest" method of accounting. The new rules replace this with the "purchase" method of accounting, which tends to give lower earnings-per-share figures on the acquiring company's income statement, according to the American Institute of Certified Public Accountants.

Another marked trend in recent annual reports is an effort to show that the corporation recognizes the importance of new and growing markets and is making specific efforts to profit from them. The directions of these efforts may be product development, acquisitions, broader marketing areas, or new methods of distribution. The opening message to shareholders discusses this purpose in many current reports, or new markets may be stressed under future plans. Growth is the active word.

Another current trend is to emphasize social problems and the responsibility of industry to help in their solution. This message is usually not included in the chief executives' letters, but it is emphasized in a separate statement by such firms as Crown Zellerbach, TRW, Inc., and RCA among others.

The question of racial integration has generally been ignored in corporate reports, even though radical changes are taking place in television and other advertising and communications media. Minority-group members are shown in the few reports that are primarily based on company personnel. However, racial problems will become a consideration for any firm that expects its annual report to influence employees and customers favorably.

Breaking the Report by Subjects

Financial data are discussed separately from the corporation's activities, products, personnel, and plans by a growing number of corporations. Some companies go as far as having two separate pieces of literature. Other devices used are sections within the report, a change in paper color for different sections, foldouts, and inserts.

Monsanto Company's 1968 conventional report was supplemented by an *Annual Review,* which is called "a book about some of the needs of man and about some of the ways Monsanto responded to these needs in 1968." Color illustrations showed the company's contributions to more successful agriculture, clean air and water, attractive housing, technical equipment, and travel and recreational facilities—many of these activities are relatively new ones in the firm's business.

Castle & Cooke sends stockholders an attractive booklet that describes and pictures its diversified activities in food, real estate, and other fields. Beneficial Standard Corporation tells about its entry into mutual funds and other financial services in the annual report and issues a booklet on real estate properties developed and managed as a separate enterprise, including income statistics and illustrations.

Northrop Corporation made an effective separation by the use of coated white paper for the first section of its 1968 report and gray, linen-finish paper for the financial data section, with a heavy blue insert between the sections. RCA's report opened with a 12-page foldout, called "a pictorial profile of RCA as it approaches its 50th anniversary in 1969." More than 600 products and services were displayed. The company suggested that the section be retained and checked at the end of ten years and predicted that many of the products will then be obsolete.

The award-winning report of International Paper Company used color photography lavishly to show operations and products and then confined the financial section to black and white. Attached to the back cover of the 1968 report was a sample of Confil, its disposable fabric.

As might be expected, products are given the most attention by firms in highly competitive industries. The reports of auto manufacturers and tobacco firms devote about half their space to illustrations of consumer products.

When the corporation adds distinctly new products or brands, this usually becomes a prominent feature of the annual report, again reflecting the desired image of growth, scientific development, and innovation.

Northrop's report discussed the firm's developments in industries other than aircraft, citing percentages of total volume in each to show the desired diversification away from one limited market. New products for communications systems and electronics were prominently illustrated and described. Standard Oil of California gave a major section to the research from which its new, antipollutant F-310 gasoline had been developed.

Most of the firms in heavy industry described and pictured new products and recently acquired divisions. Full-page illustrations and extensive copy described Dover Corporation's addition of Groen Manufacturing Company, which manufactures food processing equipment, a new venture for Dover. D. H. Baldwin Company emphasized the earnings contributions as well as the services of new dealer and public finance institutions. The reports of Armour & Company, Philip Morris, Kraftco, and others include mouth-watering color photographs of food products.

Utilities and some banks make good use of promotion for the geographical areas in which they operate; this practice is, again, in line with the tendency to talk about markets and how they are served. Showing the present and potential growth of their area is an effective way of predicting growth for the reporting corporation.

Messages from the chief executive are often the first and always a major element in the report. They generally follow a pattern, reporting success and new records where possible, outlining changes and developments, and discussing future possibilities. When the year's results have been disappointing, it is usually in the executive's letter than an explanation is made. Every corporation head can recognize the possibilities of this problem and the means by which an unfavorable record can best be made palatable by promises of change.

Other Contacts Are Available

Periodic contacts with stockholders include dividend payments and enclosures, notices of meetings and requests for proxies, quarterly or semiannual statements of earnings, reports of annual meetings, and special notices and messages. Generally these mailings are confined to essential information and are presented in a traditional, matter-of-fact style. There has been some effort to improve their readability and appearance, but many seem designed to discourage detailed perusal, particularly the requests for approval of by-laws or other corporate changes.

Almost without exception, these notices and statements are one-way communications; only in rare instances are stockholders asked for any comment or participation other than their signature on a proxy card. The few corporations that take advantage of opportunities to interest or involve their stockholders are the same firms that make excellent use of other communications.

The annual stockholders' meeting was at one time a pleasant and effective opportunity to review the year's activities and results and to discuss with investors their questions or comments. In recent years, a large number of meetings have been disrupted by individual criticisms and have been curtailed or unproductive as a result. Management cannot silence publicity-seekers or dissenters who attend the meeting, but advance planning can often limit the disturbances they cause. A complete agenda and advance notice that shareholders will be limited to one question or a total of two or three minutes of questions make it possible for the chairman to prevent long harangues.

Some corporations have moved their meetings to out-of-the-way locations to discourage attendance. Others have sought their stockholders through regional meetings and entertainment features. The nature of the company and the number of its stockholders will guide the policy on meetings.

Management may feel that special audiences are best reached in a warmer and more informal manner through company publications or house organs. Almost every company of any size at all has at least one publication, and, in general, house organs help printers keep busy across the country. House organs range from mimeographed sheets to elaborate magazines, depending on their purpose and the people for whom they are intended.

Each company publication has a specific audience that does not include the general public. The most common are for employees only and are usually modest in size and format. The traditional purpose was that of a small-town newspaper—to carry personal news of employees, describe company activities and products, and make policy announcements. There are a good many such house organs still published; they are usually edited by employees under management's supervision. However, many company publications have been modernized and combine company news with more sophisticated material. In large corporations, there may be separate publications for each plant.

Dealer publications are often used by corporations that depend on a large number of retail outlets, whether they are directly controlled or handle competitive products. Their obvious purposes are promotion of the company's products and policies and generation of goodwill. The better ones feature a soft-sell approach.

Originally *Mobil Dealer News*, published by the company's Western Division, was edited at sales headquarters and was principally concerned with new sales programs, product announcements, and warnings to keep rest rooms clean. When the division came under new direction, the new editor was a gifted newspaperman who had the courage to stand up for his policies and the ability to fit his paper to the reading interests of distributors and dealers. Written by field representatives of a public relations agency, this paper reflected the activities of the dealers. Their original promotion ideas, their community and social activities, and their hobbies were pictured and described. Cartoons and contests were featured. The result was an outstandingly popular and interesting newspaper and a high degree of participation in company programs.

A variation of the dealer publication is the periodical published for a professional field. Again, the purpose is product promotion, but publications for doctors and hospitals are more likely to suggest ideas than provide direct sales, although new products and their applications are described. These organs are prepared with professional care and are attractively illustrated and printed.

Some of the most elaborate company periodicals are those issued for stockholders. In recent years, there have been vast changes in content as well as in physical appearance. Most publications continue to concentrate on company activities, products, and plans, but newer, trend-conscious periodicals often discuss abstract concepts or deal with economic and social changes without making direct reference to the actual business of the firm. These publications have two roles: (1) to show progress and good management on the part of the corporation and (2) to develop confidence in the firm on the part of the stockholder.

Spreading the Word

Anyone who has ever moved can imagine how many notifications must be made when a corporation changes its identity. Within the organization, there must be instructions to all departments, branch offices, plants, storage facilities, perhaps retail stores or service locations. Everybody must know the new name, how it is to be used, in what form it may be reproduced, and when the change is to be made. The notification must truly penetrate every area, from executive offices to warehouses.

This internal program is usually simple compared to the notification of all outside contacts with which the corporation does business or hopes to do business—lawyers, advertising and PR agencies, product or package designers, auditors, shipping companies or forwarders, insurance agents, and banks. It must notify all transportation companies it uses, including airlines, railroads, steamship companies, trucking firms, and, possibly, taxi and ambulance services.

In the financial field, it is essential to remember, in addition, transfer agents, stock exchanges, brokers, and bonding companies. Utilities serving every office, plant, or other facility must be notified—the telephone companies, other communications firms, gas, power, steam, oil, and water suppliers.

Local, state, and federal government agencies and tax assessing and collecting bureaus must have word of the new company name and, in some instances, legal confirmation of the change. Civic, fraternal, and labor organizations, industry or trade associations, credit unions, and health plans should all be remembered.

Some of the major contacts for industrial firms are distributors, sales representatives, dealers, and service centers. Newspapers, trade or industrial journals, and financial publications can be used to advantage in spreading the news.

High on the priority list will be stockholders, depositors, policyholders, chambers of commerce, and civic groups. If the company pays for employee memberships in various organizations or clubs, they must be listed under the new name. Hotels, travel agencies, and other facilities where corporation credit has been established should also be notified.

Suppliers of raw materials, parts, subcontract services, packages, maintenance services—all types of supplies—are to be on the list. Permits, licenses, directories must be altered.

Bringing the New Image to Life

It is through the announcement of a new corporate image and the continuing campaign that the program becomes alive and reaches the people it is intended to influence. This is the function of communications—of publicity, advertising, motion pictures, meetings, and all the other channels through which the message can be carried.

Publicity is used by every company, but in many corporations, it is a hit-or-miss program, unorganized and inconsistent. Sound publicity programs can help corporate images, usually at relatively small expense.

One important advantage is that it reads as a third-party statement, not as a company claim. As a result, it may be more readily accepted than advertising that is obviously paid for.

The material for publicity and the media to which it will be offered should depend on the objectives of the image program. Financial news and publicity is a specialized field (see Chapter 8), but there are many other items that can be treated as publicity. As a rule, it is necessary to make news to get publicity. Many firms fail to recognize newsworthy material, or have no setup for its preparation and release. A program should consider all the possible types of news material and the channels through which it can be disseminated.

New products may be general news if they represent a significant development, such as a breakthrough in medicine or the first flight of an advanced airplane. If new products don't have general interest, they may be publicized in trade or industrial journals, most of which have new-product sections.

Products often get publicity about their uses, even if neither product nor use is new. Many newspapers and service magazines publish menu ideas and recipes, for which food manufacturers supply ideas and photographs. The weekly magazine sections of metropolitan papers follow the seasons and holidays, using material from the home economics departments of manufacturers. To some extent there is a tie-in of advertising and product publicity, but this is no bar to inventive publicists.

Household furnishing and appliances are given regular publicity, too, in women's magazines and the women's pages of newspapers. Often a good picture or a favorable mention can be arranged by including the product in a general article or placing it in a home to be described and illustrated. Fashion makes up a large part of the women's sections in the press.

Entertainers and sports figures are often willing to pose for the dual publicity of their activities and the products of a manufacturer.

There are several thousand publications in specialized business, professional, and trade fields that need material for weekly or monthly issues and welcome appropriate suggestions or prepared copy. These publications can become a source of inquiries and orders as well as carry the image of a progressive company.

Attention for products and recognition for a company may be obtained by providing prizes for guest participation television shows, by arranging to have products appear in movies, and as awards in service station drawings. These are usually commercial arrangements made through specialized agencies.

Companies often fail to realize that many of their activities are news *somewhere*, perhaps in the smaller papers of plant cities if not in the metropolitan press. Changes in personnel, new plants or additions, unusual uses of products—all are possibilities.

Advertising as an Image-Builder

To what extent advertising can and should be an active part of the corporate image program is a decision for each company. If a close relationship exists between the merits of its products and the identity of the corporation, the advertising will usually acknowledge it.

Institutional advertising campaigns are often a major part of a new image announcement. This advertising introduction of a new name or image is like the antibiotic treatment of an infection. If the full prescription is taken, the treatment is usually effective. If it is skimped, there can be a relapse. Just how much advertising is needed is a matter of judgment, but management will do well to use a little too much rather than not enough.

The tone of a company's advertising—the extent to which it is aggressive and competitive or restrained and conservative—will make a contribution to the corporate image, and this tone should be another policy decision. This is by no means limited to institutional advertising, as consumer copy will be seen by a much larger audience. While most people approve of a progressive—or even aggressive—attitude on the part of a company, there is an unfavorable reaction to advertising that disparages a competitor or its products.

Advertising can be particularly effective when the company is already in the news and there is an established interest in the advertising message. If the news about the corporation is favorable—such as the announcement of a new product or the discovery of oil in a new territory—the advertising can press the advantage. But most corporations are not so fortunate—when they are in the news it is because there is a strike, government action against them, or a physical disaster. Still, it is always possible to tell the company's side of the story; sometimes it becomes essential to avoid serious misunderstandings.

The extent to which the identity of a corporation can be personalized will affect its image. Most people regard large firms as cold and impersonal. Every company that does business with the public tries to replace this image with a warmer, closer relationship.

Some of the greatest image changes have taken place in banks. The marble columns of the facade and the bankers' gray of the closeted executives have been replaced by open counters, executives' desks accessible to everyone, and advertising that would have sent earlier financiers right up the granite walls.

A classic example of product advertising that created a friendly company image is "Elsie the Cow." Originally designed to represent the quality of Borden's food products, Elsie was first advertised to the medical profession. The reaction was so favorable that she became the subject of radio as well as print advertising and was a feature of Borden's exhibit at the 1939 New York World's Fair.

This success led to the exhibition of 14 Elsies in all parts of the country. People stood in line and paid money to see her in many cities. As one of the Borden men commented, "Who would ever imagine people lining up and paying a dime to see a cow?" Within ten years, surveys showed that half the people in the country identified Elsie with Borden.

A new name is usually adopted for important reasons, and usually requires an important advertising campaign. Leading corporations that have used extensive advertising for a new identity include UniRoyal, Signal Companies, Inmont, Kraftco, Chemetron, Essex International, and Amsted. Another group that changed the names but pointedly stated that "only the names have been changed," includes MPC, Amfac, and others. Adoption of a symbol by which the company is to be widely identified or the use of initials rather than the full name is also often the subject of extensive advertising in which the revised identity is usually linked with the new or broader scope of the business.

Second to the announcements of new names or symbols, the most widespread emphasis in corporate advertising has been on "change," new developments in an established company. An interesting example is Transamerica, a corporation that for many years was a conservative financial institution with a few small industrial divisions. Under new management and with new objectives in diversified fields, this firm has carried on an aggressive campaign of image building.

Continental Can has a strong campaign for the new image of this historically conservative company. To offset any idea that it is only a can company, Continental advertises 18 key divisions, from Continental Forestry Company to Continental Film & Laminate Company. All the divisions are related to the packaging industry, and Continental says they run almost as if they were separate companies.

A direct offer of information is made in the Bendix Corporation's advertisement, "What Kind of a Handle Should You Put on Bendix?" Illustrated are tool handles labeled aerospace, automotive, electronics, automation, oceanics, and multi-industry. Bendix reports this to be one of its most successful advertisements.

A number of the pioneer industrial companies have used campaigns to demonstrate their present image and to show the diversity of their operations and their continuing growth and development. Westinghouse Electric used a five-page section in *The Wall Street Journal* with each of the first four pages devoted to one segment of the business and the fifth to forecasts of developments.

Accomplishments related to major news events give corporations opportunities to display their images to advantage. The flights of Apollo spaceships gave birth to a number of advertisements showing the contributions of firms to the program.

Advertising programs aimed at consumers have been effective in building favorable images for a number of corporations. In several instances these campaigns have been successful because of their unique appeal, completely the reverse of that of hard-sell copy used in most advertisements.

The campaign for Volkswagen has pictured these cars as unattractive and unchanging in appearance over the years, but with such attractive qualities as economy, dependability, and long life. Just after the first moon trip, the company ran an ad showing a picture of the lunar module. The copy read: "It's ugly, but it gets you there." The car wasn't shown, just the logotype.

Another campaign that appealed to public interest and sympathy was Avis's claim "We Try Harder," because the company was only Number Two. Hibernia Bank in San Francisco changed the image of an old, somewhat stuffy institution to that of a modern, friendly bank through several years of illustrated puns, principally on bus and car cards. The impact and effect of such programs are often disproportionate to their cost.

Statements of corporate philosophy have been used in advertising campaigns that are far from product promotion and were designed to project the company's image.

Identification with customers has always been a favorite theme in industrial advertising, and it is becoming more popular in institutional copy. A striking example was the advertisement for Xerox in the 1968 issue of *Fortune* listing the 500 largest U.S. corporations. It read: "499 of *Fortune*'s 500 have Xerox machines. The other one makes them."

Concern with social welfare and the desire to incorporate this concern into their image appear in the institutional advertising of some firms.

A collective program of advertising, to talk about what the industry is doing and what it proposes for the future, has been published by the Institute of Life Insurance. One message concludes, "The future of our cities depends on what we do today. Now. It's a job that needs the help of business and labor and private citizens . . . inside and outside the slums." This is the kind of advertising that few firms would have used until recent years. It is not necessarily designed to build an image, but it does.

In the competitive commercial world, advertising has been a potent weapon in the announcement of a tender for another corporation's stock and in statements favoring or opposing such offers on the part of the firm being wooed. At times, more than one bidder has appeared, and financial media were used along with letters, telephone calls, and other solicitations of securities or proxies.

Movies Are Better Than Ever

Motion pictures have had a growing role in the public image programs of many corporations and will be used for more and more purposes to reach wider audiences. Films have the advantages of simultaneously employing sound, color, and movement. They do not face competition for audience attention when they are being shown, as is often the case with advertising or other presentations. If the movies are well done, they are

entertaining, instructive, or both, and can have a greater impact on selected audiences than any other medium. However, unless they are shown
on television, films can reach only limited numbers of people.

Effective motion pictures can be made in these broad categories: general public relations, public service, employee training, community relations, and marketing. Each will be designed for a specific audience, although exceptional pictures may appeal to more than one category.

It is particularly important that any picture be made to serve a definite
objective and that this be understood in advance by everyone concerned,
including corporate management, the divisions that will use the films, and
the producer. It is no longer enough to "make a picture about the company." Nobody wants to take time just to see another film. What people
want is to be informed about some subject of direct interest. This can be
their work (training films), their safety or security (public service pictures), products or services they are considering using, the activities of a
corporation in which they own stock or consider investing, or what a
company is doing in its neighborhood and other social relations.

Films may be made for the training or education of company employees, and they may be planned for dealer meetings. Some are aimed specifically at schools, and many have been designed for luncheon gatherings,
conventions, and other general audiences. Distribution may be through
the firm's public relations or sales departments or through national organizations that maintain film libraries. These public relations films are usually available without cost to the audience; a fee is paid by the corporate
owner for each showing.

Sales and training films can have only a minor, peripheral influence on
the corporate image, so the films to be considered in an image program are,
for the most part, public relations or public service films. It should be
clearly established how such pictures fit into the overall objectives, for
which audiences they will be made, how they shall be produced, and how
much they will cost.

A company that is building an image around traffic safety may want
to show a film in schools, PTA meetings, traffic courts, and before luncheon clubs, showing the problems that face drivers and how they should be
handled. If the corporation program is based on improvement of retail
outlets and the friendly service of its branches or dealers, the film would
be pointed in that direction. One of the most popular types of public relations pictures is a report on what the company is doing, the growth of its
markets, new developments in products and services, and plans for the

future. Many of these pictures are motivated by an anniversary or special event, for which they become part of the celebration. While some companies make elaborate films of this kind to show their employees and dealers the extent of their activities, such pictures can quickly become dated.

Another purpose of public relations pictures is educational—to be shown primarily in schools, but of possible interest to general audiences. Such films usually have only the opening announcement of the sponsoring corporation, with little or no identification of properties or products. Public schools use hundreds of educational films. Most of them are made by specialized producers or publishing firms and sold to the schools, but some are supplied by corporations, who indirectly gain goodwill. Industrial associations often make pictures for both schools and general audiences, and sometimes for prospective customers.

Corporate films range in quality from very good to terrible, with too high a percentage being mediocre. Attractive photography is often forced to carry a heavy-handed commentary. With the exception of simple training or sales films, few corporations produce their own pictures. There are several hundred companies and individuals throughout the country making sponsored films. Assuming a record of quality performance, the important consideration in the selection of a producer is a full understanding between client and producer of what the picture is to be and what it is expected to accomplish.

Government Contacts

There is a relatively new, and not always happy, way in which public attention is focused on a corporation that must be seriously considered by management. This is the appearance of corporate representatives before congressional committees, government agencies, or the courts.

Such an appearance is almost certain to receive extensive news coverage and possibly be given an interpretation that is not favorable to the corporate image. This is due to the fact that almost all such appearances are to answer charges of one kind or another, to defend policies and procedures against criticism, or to plead for changes in government action or legislation.

Newspapers and telecasts give prompt and generous attention to hearings before committees and bureaus. Within a given two-week period, individual corporations were in the news about one or more of the following controversial matters: regulation of air pollution devices on automobiles, excessive costs on defense contracts, proposed taxes on foundations, failure to perform on government contracts, false advertising, sexual indecency in advertising, bans on specific drugs, alleged monopoly, the alliance of business with gambling, illegal contributions to government employees, questioned acquisitions, automobile and tire safety regulations, violation of the Robinson-Patman Act, illegal loans on stocks, regulation of undersea oil drilling, discrimination in employment practices, import quotas, seizure of tuna boats, censorship of broadcast organizations, illegal arms shipments, failure to disclose required information on securities, proposed health warnings on cigarettes, award of airline routes, and expropriation of foreign properties.

It becomes essential for corporations to maintain contacts with various government bodies, to anticipate the direction of new regulations, laws, and taxes, and to make advance preparation for appearances by company executives. Obviously, not all possible contingencies can be anticipated, but an organization of staff personnel and task forces can be set up for the most effective handling of government contacts.

Personal Contacts

The image of any corporation is bound to be affected by contacts between customers and company personnel. The finest program of publicity and advertising can be completely offset by the inconsiderate or offensive actions of a company representative. This is principally true for firms that have direct contact with the public, as do retailers, banks, railroads, airlines, bus companies, home builders, finance companies, and all other service organizations. These firms must depend on their employees or their dealers to retain the goodwill of the public. Nothing else counts for much if a customer feels neglected or mistreated.

How a corporation's people behave in their relations with the public is the responsibility of employee supervisors and the merchandising organization. Management must be content with less than perfection, but they can see to it that employees take pride in the company and know what important things it is doing. This applies to factory workers as well as those who actually come into contact with customers, because everyone talks about his or her job, and what is said at home or in the neighborhood tavern reflects on the company's image.

It is particularly important that any major change in the corporation's name, product lines, affiliate companies, or policies be thoroughly understood by everyone in the organization. This can be accomplished by such established channels as meetings, films, internal house organs, bulletins, and handbooks, but however it is done, such education should be an early and important part of any new campaign.

The *manner* in which information and directions are given to employees can be as important as the facts themselves. The days of the stand-up lecture and blunt bulletin are long past, although some firms have yet to recognize this. Instead of being strictly informative (and usually dull) pictures, today's training films, either for employees or dealers, are usually humorous, light, and sometimes even emotional. They are designed to interest first, then educate.

One oil company prepared a new employee handbook to give complete information on the regulations, policies, and other relations between workers and management. It was written by the industrial relations and legal departments and was so dull and ponderous that few hardhat laborers or stenographers would have read it, let alone grasp its meaning.

The public relations department, fortunately, saw the book before it was produced and, after some controversy, got permission to revise it. In published form, it was illustrated with cartoons, written in simple, direct, and sometimes humorous language, and separated into logical sections. Perhaps it never became a best seller, but it was recognized as a helpful contribution to public, as well as industrial, relations.

Almost every large corporation depends for its prosperity on outsiders as well as on employees. They are sales representatives, distributors, dealers, brokers, export agents, and all the men and women who help move products from maker to user. The same principles and methods that are applied to employees will be effective in gaining the goodwill, cooperation, and recommendations of these key people.

What is perhaps most important in achieving the objectives of an image program is the coordination of all the methods used, the concentration on basic ideas, and the consistent use of all available communications.

7

Creating a New
Corporate Identity

As we have already defined it, a corporation's identity is the combination of all visual impressions—the appearance of properties, signs, vehicles, advertising, office interiors, stationery, products, and packages. As the basis for a new image program, new trademarks or symbols, signatures, and other identifications may be adopted.

The creation of an attractive and uniform identity can be an excellent start on many of the objectives of an image program. Within the organization, it creates a new sense of purpose for the company and shows employees how management feels and proposes to act. The introduction of a new identity soon has an effect on every part of the corporation.

To customers, investors, and the general public, the new identity is the visual expression of new attitudes. It is the most readily understood part of any image program. In addition to symbolizing the new corporate

Abstract symbols have represented companies and families since the beginning of graphics. The top illustration is the symbol of Nomura Securities of Japan, the largest financial house in the Orient. It incorporates the traditional mark of the Nomura family, established centuries ago. The Mercedes-Benz star (below) is one of the earliest and best known of the European trademarks. It is the result of gradual change and simplification over the last century.

character, the new identity usually standardizes and simplifies the way in which the company presents itself.

Corporate executives who have created new identity programs, designers, and experienced public relations consultants all emphasize the importance of these two principles:

1. *The program should be as complete as possible.* The benefits of the new identity and its promotion will be much greater, both within and outside the company, if it is used in every possible way. The new identity should be generalized rapidly, with patterns that result from the accidents of merger or acquisition giving way to the general corporate identification. Often the older marks are restricted, perhaps in legal rights overseas, in a way that makes them dated or unable to represent the company and its products.

2. *The program must have the strong support of management.* It must be carried quickly throughout the organization and implemented by meetings, bulletins, manuals, and other materials that carry the authority of top management. Once the major elements are selected, there should be no deviation in their use. Much of the value of the new program is a product of consistency.

The introduction of a new identity is nearly always initiated by top management. It will logically be developed and presented for approval by the public relations department or other designated group with the assistance of outside consultants and designers.

It is often helpful to establish an identity committee that embraces all the parts of the corporation, with representatives from each division to work with the PR or communications department. An executive usually heads such a committee and reports directly to senior management.

Soon after the program is launched, other departments should be involved in it; these would include plant operation, marketing, purchasing, advertising, patent, and legal departments. It is important to consider the progress of the new program and what the costs and procedures will be.

The appointed group or department will make the necessary contacts with others in the company and will check regularly with other firms to see how their identity programs have been handled. At this point, outside counsel or designers will make recommendations to management, and proposals from these organizations will be considered. The selection of outside consultants and the basis of their charges are discussed in Chapter 10.

When all this material is on hand, the committee will make a formal presentation to management and the board of directors and discuss the timing, problems, proposed new elements, and costs of the program. For a major change, this presentation is usually so comprehensive that it includes a review of the programs of other firms, the results of surveys, an analysis of the company's present position, and alternate plans for modernization.

A Multitude of Changes

The number of items that must be changed when a new name or symbol is introduced—and the costs of these changes—can come as a distinct shock to management. When two Pacific Coast banks were merged several years ago, just the replacement of physical properties and supplies cost nearly $1 million. Fortunately, not all firms have their names carved in marble or granite above the doors of many branches, nor do they have thousands of individual checks to be reprinted, but the expense of any new look can still be substantial.

A change in name will result in greater costs than the creation of a new symbol or logotype that is not necessarily made a part of property and office identification and can be incorporated into stationery and literature without such great expense.

The list of points at which a new look will require changes starts with physical properties that carry the company name. These include manufacturing and other plants, offices, showrooms, warehouses, retail establishments, machinery and equipment, transportation equipment, and salesmen's cars. Vehicles can include aircraft, freight cars, ships, and, for some companies, their products in use by others, such as trailers and vans.

Package identity includes labels, stickers, and tags on boxes and crates; cartons, bottles, cans, foil, or film containers; and drums and barrels. Many industrial products require unusual packaging and may be difficult to identify.

A check of stationery and forms must include the full range of sales slips, permanent records, letterheads, and envelopes—for executive headquarters, branches, divisions, and subsidiaries—business cards, order forms and confirmations, invoices and statements, reports, press releases, and data processing materials.

In a diversified corporation, it is probable that a new system will kill off the traditional trademarks and symbols, which are treasured and

This corporate checklist of all points of identification is a guide to the establishment of the new identity system.

	Column A		Column B	
1. Packaging	LABELS		CANS	
	STICKERS		DRUMS	
	TAGS		CLOSURES	
	CARTONS		DISPLAYS	
	BOXES AND CRATES		OTHER	
	BOTTLES			
2. Advertising & Promotion	NEWSPAPERS		POSTERS	
	MAGAZINES (CONSUMER)		MERCHANDISING AIDS	
	MAGAZINES (TRADE & BUSINESS)		RESEARCH REPORTS	
	TELEVISION		GIVEAWAYS AND GIMMICKS	
	BOOKLETS & BROCHURES		OTHER	
	CATALOGUES			
3. Signage	OFFICE ENTRANCE		DOORS — INTERNAL	
	PLANT ENTRANCE		PLANT INDENTIFYING — EXTERNAL	
	SHOWROOM AND/OR RETAIL OUTLETS		OTHER	
4. Institutional Literature	ANNUAL REPORT		EMPLOYEE BOOKLETS	
	LEGAL DOCUMENTS		NOTICES AND BULLETINS	
	HOUSE ORGANS		OTHER	
5. Stationery and Forms	EXECUTIVE OFFICE LETTERHEADS/ENVELOPES		INVOICES AND STATEMENTS	
	DIVISIONAL LETTERHEADS/ENVELOPES		PRESS RELEASE FORMS	
	BRANCH OFFICE LETTERHEADS/ENVELOPES		REPORT FORMS	
	CALLING CARDS		OTHER	
	ORDER FORMS			
6. Buildings and Equipment (stationary)	PLANTS — EXTERNAL APPEARANCE		SHOWROOM DECOR AND FURNISHINGS	
	OFFICES — EXTERNAL APPEARANCE		MACHINERY AND PRODUCTION EQUIPMENT	
	RETAIL OUTLETS — EXTERNAL APPEARANCE		OTHER	
	OFFICE DECOR AND FURNISHINGS			
7. Transportation	TRUCKS		FREIGHT & TANK CARS	
	COMPANY CARS		MATERIALS HANDLING EQUIPMENT	
	COMPANY AIRCRAFT		OTHER	
	SHIPS			
8. Company Identification	TRADEMARKS		SPECIAL PRODUCT NAMES	
	TRADE NAMES		COMPANY COLORS	
	LOGOTYPES		PRODUCT COLORS	
	SLOGANS		OFFICIAL TYPE STYLES	

fought for by some people in the company. Management may hesitate to set up a program that requires immediate changes in all parts of the company identity. Usually, however, the additional cost of prompt execution is more than offset by the added impact of the campaign and the economies that follow standardization.

Costs can be estimated in advance for any individual firm's program, but there is no basis for setting a general range of costs. The factors vary so widely from one company to another that the budget could range from $50,000 for a simple design change to more than $1 million for replacement of physical properties. Fees for consultants and designers must be included, as well as the time of company personnel and overhead. For manufacturers of consumer products, the cost of promotion to introduce a new name or symbol is usually greater than the expense of physical changes.

Any firm that identifies its products or company name on thousands of retail outlets, such as a petroleum or tire company, has the added expense of setting up uniform signs that can be used under any conditions. These companies have paint manuals that specify the standard lettering and colors that must be used by company and independent outlets.

Trademarks Can Be Critical

Most plans for the introduction of a new corporate look place the trademark, the printing of the name, and the colors used among the principal considerations. Identification of the firm and its products will be made by these trademarks, trade names, special product names, symbols, and signatures.

Any change in the trademark becomes a concern of the legal and patent departments. A new or revised trademark will have to be registered, in the United States and foreign countries as well, to prevent encroachment. A trade name cannot be registered, but it usually wins a degree of recognition that will be ruled exclusive and not to be directly copied.

Symbols are more controversial. If they are not unique (for example, if they are simply company initials), they may be so similar to others that they cause competition and confusion. Companies with foreign business take care to use symbols or names that can be recognized and understood anywhere, are not difficult to read, and are not offensive in any country.

Coca-Cola has a bottle and name that have become familiar around the world. Singer has established an identity for sewing machines and other appliances in many countries.

In foreign promotion, many products have a visual presentation that does not depend on the use of any language and establishes the product internationally. Along many Mediterranean beaches, there are signs for Coppertone, Plough, Inc.'s tanning oil. They show the same illustration used in the United States, that of a dog pulling the bathing suit off a little girl. There is no language problem, the message is evident to everyone.

The patent department in one corporation has set these strictures for present or future trade names and trademarks:

1. Maximum exclusiveness of trade name and trademark.
2. Careful controls on the use of the corporate name and symbol to provide uniformity and continuity in all media.
3. Careful consideration of legal problems confronting the use of the corporate name and trademark in associated companies.
4. A continuing program of policing the unauthorized use of the company name and trademark to minimize or forestall encroachment.
5. Registration of the most valuable trademarks in foreign countries to protect the corporation's rights to use such marks in a worldwide market.

Trends in modern design have been toward the contemporary, the simple, the highly recognizable, and the uncluttered. Good symbols are impersonal, general enough for worldwide use, and not limited to any special appeal or audience. In general, the new symbol designs are abstract; they make no attempt to represent products, because many firms are so diverse that their products could not be blanketed in one design. This principle has been basic to the design of products, packages, and even buildings. Unfortunately, as the use of abstract symbols multiplies, they come to look so similar that it is hard to distinguish among them.

One advertising executive, after reviewing the presentations of several designers for the identity campaign of a client, commented that it would be possible to make one overlay fit most of the designs and recommendations received. He questioned the designers' high charges for "research" when their programs for several firms are so similar.

To check the similarity of advertising campaigns that have announced new identities, a number of elements were compared in 25 advertisements. In 14 of them, the headline typeface was Helvetica. Others used similar or modified type styles. In 11 of the advertisements, a three-column format was used; and in 8, type was set flush on the left margin and ragged on the right. The most common element of style was placement of the company name and symbol. Twelve campaigns used illustrations that occupied half or more of the space.

One designer points out that management should be cautioned against stereotyped presentations, programs that are similar to others, temporary fads in style, elements that can date the company's image, and names and symbols that are not compatible with good judgment.

In a paper on package design and identity symbols, Frederick Siebel, a New York designer, considers at length the problems of creating a campaign that is contemporary without becoming another "look-alike." He says,

> The truth is, that when we say a design is contemporary we are saying that it is the idiom that is currently fashionable. A corollary is that what is fashionable today was not fashionable yesterday and probably won't be tomorrow.
>
> It is so hard to achieve an identity in this world—once you have it, why then try to look like everybody else? What is the benefit of being clean and modern—if clean and modern is all you are? Everybody else can be clean and modern, too—and you will all blend together like the new buildings on Park Avenue that look so much alike. Isn't it better to be known and noticeable and distinctive and remembered?
>
> Ivory Soap was 99 and 44/100 percent pure back at the turn of the century. When it rained 50 years ago, Morton's salt was already pouring from the shaker under the little girl's arm. Prudential had the strength of Gibraltar back in the days when the sun hadn't set on the British Empire. The flying red horse was in orbit long ago before the first jet plane got off the ground. (I'm aware that he was recently shot down in cold blood, but as an eyewitness to the shooting I'm willing to swear that up to the time of death he hadn't even broken a leg.)
>
> To remove every hint of personality, every trace of individuality, and to arrive at a thing that is somehow "pure"—when you remove all the frills, when you clean up all the fussiness, when you eliminate every little personal whim and conceit—when you root out all the imperfections of design from a package or a corporate symbol—it is tantamount to dressing all the people in the same shapeless outfits.
>
> The majority of the new corporate symbols are typographic—basically coined words or abbreviations. The idea being that since the combination of letters involved has no meaning it cannot be misunderstood. I

might point out that until these coined words are given meaning—if ever—they will be meaningless to people who come in contact with them.

The plain fact is that the old corporate symbols, which—like the flying red horse—are being so hastily discarded today, were developed in the first place as substitutes for names that a largely illiterate people could not read in any language.

There is just one more point that needs to be made here. And that is that at the very moment when the trend in corporate design is becoming more pristine, more sterile, more conformist—the consumer, the one everybody is trying to influence, is busily staging a rebellion against this sterility. Pure design? He's having none of it. For him, today, you cannot make design eclectic enough.

To make possible improvements in its identification without losing the recognition established over many years, Standard Oil Company of California opened an investigation in 1967. Two years later the result, after months of design, testing, and comparison, was a new Chevron trademark. The new design is instantly recognized as "Chevron." As compared to the old design, it has a brighter red and blue in a double stripe, separated by a narrower white strip and topped with the word "Standard" or "Chevron" in distinctive lettering.

In actual use at service stations and elsewhere, the upper chevron is blue and the lower chevron is red.

Around this central design is built a companywide identity system that will put the Chevron symbol on everything from service stations to oil cans. In time, the trademark will be used for every visual contact, including vehicles, stationery, advertising, packages, facilities signs, and credit cards. The program will extend over several years, eventually covering about 35,000 outlets. In established Chevron territory, larger, brighter signs will replace the old signs; where other names such as Caltex have been used, there is completely new identification. The program was opened in Europe, where new signs were erected at 8,000 outlets.

An introduction of the new trademark, as announced in the company's *Bulletin,* concluded with this statement:

> A sound corporate identity program can't afford to be just a cosmetic project. Unless it is functional and represents the company as it really is, it's bad design and bad business.

> Moreover, such a program also has a catalytic effect; no matter how well a company is performing, proper identification can frequently improve performance.

Programs Can Be Extended

A company with many properties and a well-established trademark or symbol may decide to make changes in stages (1) to give the organization a chance to establish the new identity through a gradual replacement and (2) to write off the costs of modernization over a period of several years. Such a program would call for converting to new signs, new stationery, and possibly new packages as existing stocks were used up. This kind of campaign does not permit advertising or publicity for the new look, but it is the only arrangement available to firms with limited funds and extensive properties.

Contrasting policies in the timing of physical change have been seen in the handling of two California bank mergers. When Security First National acquired Pacific National of San Francisco to form Security Pacific National Bank, which had nearly 400 branches in southern California, there was a problem of signs and other identification. The bank decided to handle changes on a normal replacement basis, rather than all at one time. The new name was immediately used in San Francisco and in other branches as they were opened, but it was instituted in old ones only as they would normally have been refurbished. The same policy was adopted for checks, passbooks, and other materials, which were used up rather than discarded.

Crocker-Citizens National Bank, another merger of northern and southern California institutions, replaced signs and other identifying materials immediately, almost as soon as the ink was dry on the merger agreement.

When American Can Company adopted a new corporate signature several years ago, a manual was prepared and circulated throughout the organization. The campaign was designed to show the new and varied activities and products of the firm, which had for many years been regarded as just a can manufacturer. The campaign had good support from the executives and division managers, but no effort was made to rush new signs onto company property and other facilities. As opportunities for replacement came along, changes were made.

Usually, identity manuals call for prompt changes in all physical properties and immediate use of the new look for advertising, packaging, stationery, and other items. Most manuals permit little or no variation, particularly in the style and color of a new symbol or the logotype of a new name.

When Weyerhaeuser Company decided to drop the word "Forest" from its name, management took this occasion to introduce a new identity, for which a symbol and logotype system were designed. The new identification was planned for every possible use on all properties and printed materials, although the program was gradual rather than immediate. The company's employee publication made the first announcement:

> Corporate identity is a means of influencing the image that the public holds of a company. In the past, the public has not had a consistent, clear image of Weyerhaeuser because of the many symbols, names, and type styles used in connection with the company name on products, trucks, letterheads, business cards, water towers—wherever the name appeared.

> Under the new corporate identity system, it is expected that consistent use of the company name within a carefully outlined procedure whenever the name is used as the company signature will help to project an image of the integrity of the company to the public mind. . . .

> The main reason given for the change is that the company's scope of activity and variety of products made the old name too limiting to be really descriptive of the company's true nature. It was also pointed out

The old Weyerhaeuser symbols (*a* and *b*) have given way to the new abstract symbol (*c*).

a

b

c

Weyerhaeuser's instruction manual illustrates distortions and improper uses of its symbol.

Squared base

Improper radius

Pointed tips

Improper angle

Curved sides

Sides too thin

Don't embellish

Don't shadow or outline

Don't use two colors or border

Don't split with background

Don't combine positive and negative

Don't overprint

Don't use a background shape

Don't use as a decorative device

by the design firm that the combination of the old company name with division and product names made long and unwieldy terms.

The new symbol is the cornerstone for the system. . . . The symbol's job is to catch the eye and attract it to the name. To do this, the symbol must be attractive, unique, indicative of the forest products industry, and must be adaptable to being printed in a wide variety of sizes and on materials varying from paper to plywood.

To implement the new identity, an instruction manual was prepared and distributed that described the new look and its applications to each type of material. In addition to illustrating correct usage, the manual warns against ways in which an artist may distort the symbol and cautions both designers and printers that the symbol cannot appear in just any manner that an art director can devise.

This manual, the *Corporate Identity Guide,* has been an active means of communication, with supplements issued as new or better means of identification are developed. Everything possible has been done to make changes simple by establishing sources of supply for signs and other materials. Standard colors have been adopted for buildings, vehicles, and other display areas, and a national contract has been arranged by which paints are supplied. The standardization of colors, sign materials, decals, and stationery has cut costs.

This identity change has been a gradual program, with signs and other materials replaced as needed, but management has emphasized that all possible opportunities for change should be promptly used. Announcements of new materials, reports of applications, and other instructions on corporate design are issued in the bulletins from the public affairs department. The cooperation of the entire organization has been continually enlisted. For example, one bulletin put it this way:

Practically everyone in the company is responsible for helping build an effective corporate identity system. How we look in the eyes of the public depends on how well we maintain our equipment and buildings, how we package our products, as well as how our signs and advertising look. The public affairs department is responsible for providing overall direction to the corporate identity program and, whenever possible, developing standard materials. This will make your jobs easier—and your dollars go farther.

MacMillan Bloedel Limited of Vancouver, Canada, is another growing firm that has modernized its corporate identity and implemented the program with a complete manual, printed in the new corporate color and including "a total design project encompassing every aspect of our operations that is on public view." The program was introduced to the organization with this statement.

> Our new trademark symbolizes the kind of company we are: the spirit of the way we think and operate, our people, and our products.

> In the literal sense it is a distinctively styled "M" letterform that encloses two coniferous tree shapes. Beyond this, however, its graphic configuration embodies and projects certain characteristics that are synonymous with what MacMillan Bloedel Limited stands for and what we produce.

In addition to the new symbol and the authorized presentations of the corporate and divisional names, the manual shows the improper uses of these identities. Such uses include any change in the symbol, such as its combination with circles or other forms, and forbids shadowing, transpo-

Two authorized layouts shown in the instruction manual of MacMillan Bloedel Limited. The manual indicates exactly six permissible sizes, some larger, some smaller than the ones shown here.

sitions, outlining, or tilting. Examples are given of how name and symbol should appear on advertising logotypes, stationery, cards, forms, signs, equipment, and packages.

As Boise Cascade's new symbol (the company uses the term "hallmark") was introduced, instructions were given as to the relative size of the design and name in all company identifications. Westinghouse Electric Corporation had a new typeface designed for its name and specified which typefaces might be used with the new signature. Other firms instruct divisions or subsidiaries as to how they are to incorporate their names into the parent company signature.

An interesting development in the creation of new corporate images has been the branding of materials that for many years were never identified. Most finished lumber is now marked with the company symbol. Oranges, bananas, and avocados are branded; cuts of meat carry company identification; produce is trimmed, packaged, and branded.

Packages Are Part of Identity

Packages can have a part in the corporate image and identity programs, although this is not their primary function. Consumer packages are designed to attract customers, as well as to deliver the product in a convenient form and good condition. Industrial packaging is mainly for product protection and easy identification, and is sometimes used to provide instruction.

When a new identity is being established, all the packages should be evaluated to see whether they should be included in the program. In many lines of consumer goods, the company and the product are closely associated.

Some corporations have the problem of adapting an emblem to widely varying products that may have been brought together through mergers. The new company may be in heavy industrial machinery and electronic components or in steel pipe and silk stockings. Sometimes no attempt is made at uniform corporate identification, leaving the products of each division under their original names.

Reciprocal business is important to many corporations, and this exchange of business increases with the size of the amalgamations. This is another reason why divisions and product lines should be identified with

Libby is believed to be the oldest food brand still in existence. The first Libby label appeared in 1875. Package changes were made at intervals introducing the Libby script, showing illustrations of raw products, and giving recipes. The bolder script now in use first appeared in the 1930s, when illustrations were changed from raw to processed products. Finally a new design was adopted featuring the new pennant, modernized product illustrations, and details about the contents. It is now used on more than 300 products.

the corporation—so that their present ownership is apparent to anyone doing business with any part of the firm.

In the same industry, two companies may have opposite policies about tying products to the parent. Some of the drug firms, such as Lilly and Merck, base much of their appeal on the firm's name; others—Plough, Inc., for example—advertise and market a wide line of products but make little attempt to relate them to each other or to the corporation, in consumer promotion.

Involving the Entire Organization

New identification programs are often introduced through meetings within the organization as well as by films, bulletins, and manuals. Responsibility for checking compliance with new styles and symbols is established by executive order and usually monitored by management and public relations staffs. All suppliers of packages, signs, literature, or advertising must be made familiar with the program and given samples and instructions.

As has been discussed, the best control results from bringing everyone into the program, so that it is understood and appreciated. This measure is usually supplemented by a check throughout the organization to make sure that no deviations take place.

During the implementation and policing of a program, the cooperation of the purchasing department is important. When this department has complete and detailed information on all identity specifications, such as typefaces, colors, and package designs, and knows that management will enforce the instructions completely, there can be no question of changing these standards.

There may be divergent views on signs, printed materials, plant colors, or other identifications in any large corporation. If there is not total control, a division or a department may not always conform to specifications. This could happen with something as important as a plant sign or as minor as the color of a report folder.

Identity standardization may appear expensive when it is put into effect, but over a period of time, it can result in important economies. A large corporation that has set specific colors for plant exteriors and interiors, offices, machinery, and vehicles can negotiate contracts for paint at substantial savings. Standard formats, type, and color specifications result in printing economies. Delays are avoided and jobs made easier for purchasing personnel, maintenance crews, and outside contractors.

Designing the Annual Report

More and more firms are hiring specialized organizations to design their annual reports. These specialists may be design studios, advertising agencies, or public relations people. In concert with these specialists, management should decide whether the report is to be conservative or contemporary, to what extent it will discuss products, personnel, social comment; whether the use of colors and illustrations will be formal or highly imaginative. Management need not be concerned with production details, but the overall appearance and character of the report should be senior management's responsibility. No other element of the image program represents the corporation to the same extent as the annual report does.

In appearance, reports range from nondescript to flamboyant. The use of color photography can be conventional or psychedelic, occasionally so far out that the subject is hard to recognize. Imaginative illustrations make otherwise prosaic subjects interesting; the photo of a piece of equipment in dramatic action is more effective than a catalog type of picture; people working at their jobs look more convincing than posed portraits.

As in other creative efforts, there is a limit to the use of unusual effects if they are to be understood and in good taste. Some reports are so involved with dividers, gatefolds, inserts, and other interrupting devices, as well as faddish art and photography, that they are difficult to read and comprehend. Some stockholders also feel that the conspicuous expenditure of so much money is unnecessary and perhaps not in keeping with the desired image of the corporation.

There is little to recommend the general use of numerous posed photographs of officers and directors, often in groups around a table. Why management should feel that shareholders and other interested members of the financial community want to examine page after page of such pictures is hard to imagine. Some companies do use worthwhile action photos of personnel, but many persist in the traditional shots that are as obsolete as illustrations of factory smokestacks.

Too many annual reports discourage readers by using type that is too small, set too wide, and unbroken by subheads or illustrations, or, especially, printed over color or in reverse in white on black. These errors are not typical of reports created by designers as a rule, but unbroken masses of type are occasionally found in otherwise good reports.

Extensive organization charts are still favored by certain firms, possibly based on the wishful thinking that the names and titles of dozens of people will impress investors. More effective means of showing extensive activities include the worldwide maps of petroleum companies or construction firms. The size of a corporation is not necessarily reflected in the size and elaborateness of its annual report. Some of the major companies use simple formats.

Print Magazine publishes a yearly survey of the best annual reports from its study of 500 major corporations. Its judgment is based primarily on physical appearance:

> Of the approximately 500 reports we see annually, about 30 or 40 turn out to be first rate, another 60 or so partially successful, about 35 to 40 incredibly bad, and the rest mediocre. . . . In other words, at least three out of four annual reports produced today still communicate ineptly. We make a special effort each year to solicit reports from companies which we have reason to believe will submit good ones. Thus, if anything, our figures and percentages are rather on the optimistic side.

> A great many reports are severely hampered visually by their misuse of photography. Fewer photos, more effectively presented, would help the results enormously. Hasn't the message gotten across that the most exciting photography in annual reports has a natural, documentary look?

8

Convincing the
Financial Community

THE financial welfare of a corporation, as represented by its ability to obtain capital for expansion and to persuade the investing public to accept its securities, may be the principal concern of management and the major objective of a new or improved image program.

This financial position, obviously, depends on the performance of the corporation, its sales volume and profit margin, and, particularly, the *trends* of these statistics. No management can long retain a favorable image in the financial community for a business that is not successful. At best, there may be an opportunity to present a new picture when the firm has turned a corner or changed its management.

If results are left to outside interpretation, changes in opinion will be slow. Inertia holds back new attitudes on any facet of a corporate image. More and more companies are working hard to change their reputations as soon as they have sound progress to report. They are aggressive in their image programs, vocal about improvements. But this is not the blatant and sometimes misleading propaganda of promoters, it is the sound, strong presentation of new facts and policies.

The Power of the Financial Community

The men who evaluate each corporation are bankers, brokers, underwriters, analysts, consultants, publishers, and all others who arrange and control the issuance and exchange of securities and the financing of industry. It is a diversified but cohesive group, relatively small but tremendously powerful. What the financial community does and says is instantly reflected in quotations for securities on the exchanges and over the counter, and in the media that serve this special field. Few activities are as closely regulated as banking and securities investment, although this protection for customers and investors is relatively new.

There is overlapping of activities among the large organizations in this community. Investment bankers are also brokers in that they handle the exchange of securities on a commission basis, even though their principal function may be to underwrite new issues. Brokers, of course, distribute new securities as well as supervise daily market transactions. Commercial banks are basically interested in loans, ranging from small personal accommodations to the extended financing of giant enterprises at home and abroad.

Surrounding the central core of the market are thousands of securities analysts, consultants, and brokers who are in direct contact with the individuals and institutions holding securities and other investments. Financial institutions, one of the fast-growing segments of the community, include mutual funds, pension funds, insurance companies, educational institutions, trusts, and foundations.

This is the community to which financial public relations will be directed. Communications with these people will make up an important part of the corporate image program of any firm that has securities in the hands of the public, that anticipates the need of private or public financing, or that may be interested in acquiring other companies or merging with them.

Financial PR can be a separate program, but it is often part of the general promotion campaign. When separate, it may be under the administration of the treasurer or vice-president of finances rather than the public relations or advertising department. In this case, it will usually have its own budget and, as we shall see, its own special counsel.

The objectives of financial PR are usually close to the overall plans of the company, although the targets and media may be selective. For some firms, financial considerations will be of primary importance; for others, with consumer products or services, this may be a secondary campaign. Some occasions call for a highly intensive program.

When objectives of the overall corporate image program are set up, decisions should be made on priorities and allocations for both general and financial campaigns. Within the financial community, there may be specific target audiences. For some corporations, one all-inclusive campaign may reach both customers and investors. This is a logical approach for a few firms but is not a general practice.

Some large corporations have never provided the financial community with any information except the mandatory data in annual reports and statements to the exchanges and SEC. Others that were silent for years have now created strong programs, usually in order to revise their image. A relatively small number have kept their names before the investing public for many years and have an unusually high degree of recognition as a result.

Older executives have often been reluctant to change their policies of silence. They fail to recognize that the investing public and regulatory agencies are now demanding more complete information. Still more important, they do not realize that under present competition it is not enough merely to have a good record, it is essential that the record become widely known.

More than one corporation, including some of the large conglomerates, has enjoyed a rising market for its stock that was based on growth through acquisitions and the public's expectation of continued improvement in earnings. When these earnings failed to grow at the expected rate and stock prices fell, the managements began to consider for the first time how their firms should be presented and rushed into new corporate image programs. Other firms have, in contrast, worked consistently for public acceptance through the intelligent use of financial public relations.

Changing Attitudes Toward the Public

Firms that are subject to rate regulation, such as transportation companies and public utilities, have always worked, with varying success, to gain investor acceptance as one buffer against federal and state commissions. The railroads have had a generally poor image, reflected both in lack of patronage and the price of their securities.

In June 1970, President William B. Johnson discussed with security analysts the change from the Illinois Central Railroad to IC Industries, Inc. He reported that in 1969 IC Industries had revenues of $736 million, with $311 million from recently acquired manufacturing operations.

"The public be damned" was a common attitude of business in the last century, and criticism of industry was general. For example, John C. Calhoun, American statesman (1782–1850), stated that "a power has risen up greater than the people themselves, consisting of many and various and powerful interests, combined into one mass and held together by the cohesive power of the vast surplus in the banks."

The "trust-busting" period of President Theodore Roosevelt was acclaimed by the public, but in the last generation there have been amalgamations and concentrations of industry unheard of in his administration. Business has tried to educate the public to gain acceptance of its practices and prevent more stringent regulation. Any general acceptance of business has largely resulted from the favorable reputation of individual firms.

Significant changes are taking place in industry's attitude toward the public. In the past, the major objectives have been the growth of sales and earnings and consequent improvement in stock quotations. Today ownership has moved rapidly into the hands of the public, and the executives are professional managers, rarely major owners.

This class of professional managers is, in part, a result of the rapid growth of corporations and the urgent need for executives. Business schools have supplied young men who are able to move quickly into positions of responsibility. The use of data processing and the necessity of understanding computers have accelerated the corporate trend toward young, aggressive executives. There has been a good deal of movement by these young men, who are usually looking for rapid advancement.

In some areas, business has not been so effective in molding opinion in its favor. There are strong feelings against major industry among the faculties of some universities, where teachers may advocate greater regulation of business, dissolution of large corporations, and restrictions on advertising and marketing. In certain universities, there is a feeling on the part of some graduates that teaching, government service, or social work is preferable to a business career.

These rapid changes in the business world and the conflicting public attitudes accentuate the need for sound financial public relations. One vital result may be the effect on legislators and government officials, with whom contact by corporations has become a major part of forward planning.

To many corporate managements, the price of company securities is highly important, and virtually every executive watches these quotations. The success of the company's operations is the basis for its stock prices, but everybody in the financial world recognizes that quotations are also influenced by corporate news, publicity, advertising, and the statements of its management.

Financing Is Essential

Many firms depend on additional stock or bond issues to finance continuing expansion, and such underwritings are more successful if existing securities have been good investments. Management is also concerned when key personnel have stock options, the future right to buy company securities at a specified price. Unless quotations go up, there is no inducement for the option holder; if they go down, he becomes definitely unhappy. Stock purchase plans for employees, with partial payment by the company, are common among large corporations, presumably because such plans will provide a substantial part of retirement income. Here again, higher stock prices are not just desirable, they are essential, or employees will be disposed to leave.

For any corporation seeking to acquire other firms or to enter a merger, it is highly important to have a favorable stock position—that is, a relatively high ratio of stock price to earnings. Many seek tax-free mergers through the exchange of common stocks, and it is apparent that a firm with a low price-earnings ratio is at a disadvantage. Alternatives are acquisition by payment of cash, convertible securities, or warrants. Acceptance of any of these depends on the esteem in which the corporation is held, an indication of future growth in earnings.

During the volatile market swings of 1968 and 1969, numbers of announced mergers were called off when the price of one or another stock dropped sharply. Other mergers were postponed, and the terms were altered to bring the exchange to its original level. This was particularly true of stocks that had extreme price-earnings ratios. When it became apparent that some of these high-flying firms could not maintain their rate of growth and earnings, they dropped in public favor.

There is no implication here that any program of financial public relations can replace increased growth and profits by the corporation. Nor will publicity and advertising bring applicants for merger, unless there are benefits to be gained. But a sound program can definitely influence investors, bring support to a company when it is needed, attract the interest of others in the financial community, and improve the bargaining power of a prospective buyer.

The importance of being recognized when seeking acquisitions is illustrated by the case of an industrial corporation that had concentrated on heavy equipment and military supplies. The firm had a good record of growth and earnings and was in sound financial condition but had never made any effort to publicize its accomplishments. The price of the stock had been flat.

Seeking growth and diversification through acquisitions, the chairman of this firm made a trip through industrial centers to visit possible sellers. The trip was singularly unsuccessful. He found that more remote companies knew nothing about his firm and had little interest in discussing a merger.

When the chairman returned to headquarters, a reorganization took place and all management people began to take an active interest in financial public relations. An agency was retained and a campaign opened. Over several years, the company has doubled and redoubled in size, largely through acquisitions. Again, no one claims that this success is solely the result of good financial PR, but everyone in the company is aware that the improved image was of substantial help.

New technological developments and new products, often in electronics, aerospace, and power generation fields, have been exploited by hundreds of new companies. Most were first known only in their own localities or in limited fields of industry, but a number jumped to national prominence. In almost every instance, well-conceived programs of publicity and promotion of these firms attracted interest.

Shareholders Are Often Neglected

There is reason to believe that most corporations overlook opportunities to enlist the support of their shareholders—opportunities both to enhance the corporate image and to obtain direct business.

In one continuing study of investor relations, more than 200 dividend-paying, publicly held corporations have been checked for 17 years. Only 11 have promoted the company's products or services to shareholders or asked for their suggestions or recommendations, enlisted their help in research, or encouraged further investment in the firm's securities except in required communications.

The most important contact with shareholders, as has already been discussed, is the mandatory annual report. The other promotion contact is the customary letter from the president or chairman to the new shareholder. This letter invariably welcomes the investor, usually calls attention to products or services, and sometimes gives a brief history of the company. Most such letters are friendly, few are inspiring, nearly all are the last contact the shareholder will have with the chief executive.

Assuming that the firm is a good investment for the shareholder, where can a company find people who are as well disposed to be friendly and helpful?

Mutual funds have an advantage, and they are making full use of their contacts with their shareholders. They propose that dividends and capital returns be used to buy additional shares, and they offer plans for regular investments by periodic payments. These are among the reasons that the funds have gained numerous investors and a rapidly increasing share of the public's total investment. Their methods are not available to corporations, but there is no sound reason that investments cannot be indirectly influenced by any firm.

A good many firms buy advertisements on financial pages to announce their dividends; they may point out that "this is the 69th year of consecutive dividend payments." There is no evidence that similar statements, such as the fact that dividends have been increased a certain number of times in recent years, are ever attached to shareholders' checks. Usually the only enclosure is a form for change of address.

Effective Methods Are Available

Corporate advertising is an important part of the program and budget of many firms, particularly those with new images or identities to be established. Only one instance (by the SAFECO Corporation) is recorded of the enclosure of image-building advertising in any mailing to shareholders.

Boise Cascade Corporation, a rapidly growing producer of building materials and related products, is one of the most active in making contact with its stockholders. At regular intervals, the investor receives the *Boise Cascadian*, an informal, illustrated magazine that contains reproductions of advertisements, articles on various divisions of the company, and the corporate philosophy. In one issue, advertising was discussed as follows:

> You have seen our corporate advertising many times. . . . Perhaps you have wondered about it—why it talks about concepts, rather than what our company does. The fact is that we have product advertising, a great deal of it, to tell people what we do. Our corporate advertising, on the other hand, is designed to tell people how we think—the kind of people we are.
>
> True, this is considerably different from most of the other corporate advertising we see. But, then, Boise Cascade is a unique kind of company. We've always done things a bit differently, right from the start, and, we hope, a little better. It all comes down to our philosophy, our attitudes toward people, and the way we approach our job. This is what we convey in our corporate advertising.
>
> These are honest beliefs we express in our advertising. We hope they are helping people to understand the uniqueness of Boise Cascade, and to see us as we really are: a company dedicated to creating greater value.

That people are a principal concern is again emphasized in the annual report, which gives more space to photographs of employees and reproduction of advertisements than to financial records. Boise Cascade personalizes its image and the people who run the company at every opportunity. The corporate film is based on the significance of people. Holiday greetings were a photographic calendar booklet with an introductory message from President R. V. Hansberger.

As Castle & Cooke has grown from its earlier Hawaiian identity to include real estate and food divisions on the mainland, it has actively promoted both image and products to its stockholders. Each new investor receives an attractive sample case of such food products as Dole Pineapple, Bumble-Bee Tuna, and Royal Macadamia Nuts. Enclosed with the letter of welcome to new stockholders is a full-color brochure describing the activities and products of Castle & Cooke and reviewing the history and development of the 200-year-old organization.

American Sugar takes advantage of the interest in unusual holiday gifts to promote direct orders for its Domino American Heritage Basket. A colorful booklet proposes sending "this oval, oaken basket for Christmas" and suggests uses for the basket.

Monopoly companies that are dependent to some extent on the attitude of the public have, in some instances, developed excellent investor programs. For example, Arizona Public Service, which covers all of the state north of Tucson, has a program in which each year the president, treasurer, and other officers spend the better part of a month in a round of stockholder meetings—at breakfast, lunch, and dinner—in most of the communities around the state. They meet the people who have invested in their corporation and tell its progress. Arizona Public Service also flies investment bankers to Arizona for a two-day session each year to discuss current results and forecasts.

Shareholders Can Contribute Suggestions

If the company wants to increase the uses of a product, shareholders might be given a chance to offer suggestions. Everybody likes to get into the act, particularly when the act is an opportunity to take part in the affairs of a large organization. In view of the widespread sampling and demonstration of the many new products sent to "boxholder" or "occupant," there seems to be an opportunity for more accurately directed promotion wherever a friendly relationship exists. Corporations could gain from the experience of retailers, who seldom send *any* mailing without offering merchandise. If it is effective to solicit business when sending a bill, it might be more so with a dividend.

Most firms overlook the fact that about half of all common stock is owned by women. The companies make no distinction among members of their corporate family, although it is recognized that women often invest with different motives than masculine investors.

When proposed revisions of federal tax laws included changes in the depletion allowances for oil companies, some companies sent urgent letters to stockholders asking them to write to senators and congressmen in favor of the industry's position. One corporate letter called the proposed changes "ill-founded, politically expedient, and misinformed."

While further controls on cigarette advertising were before Congress, the American Tobacco Company sent its shareholders a booklet that outlined the industry's position on eight questions and a letter from Chairman Robert B. Walker. A six-page letter was sent to all stockholders by Ling-Temco-Vought, asserting that conglomerates are not a menace to free competition and should not be subject to any controls and restrictions that are not applied to other firms.

A number of corporations have written and advertised to their stockholders in regard to publicly announced tender offers. These tenders may be made without the cooperation of the second firm. This may reflect the fact that managers and owners are two different groups; the stockholders may be induced to sell at a premium price, but the executives resist the loss of control and their good jobs. Both aspects of the situation may be publicized to stockholders. The image of the tendering corporation can be a sizable factor in the decisions of investors.

Potential investors make up another major target for financial public relations. Mutual and pension funds, insurance companies, educational institutions, and other large investors are particularly important to the market position of the firm's securities. The performance of the company —its record of growth and profits—is the basis for selection by these investors. Management should use all means to bring this information and the forecasts of future developments to the market's attention. Reaching the financial community through direct contacts as well as written communications is also important.

Focusing the Program

The possible accomplishments of a complete and continuous financial PR program are so great that the campaign should have full consideration and management support. Definite objectives can be set up and worked toward, but corporate management should recognize the limitations of any program. It is often futile to spend time and money on propaganda when conditions are unfavorable. This does not mean that nothing should be done, as it is critical to retain respect, if not favor; but the campaign will be largely defensive until the corporate problems are solved.

Management should rely on research to formulate a program that is within the range of possibilities. The first requirement is an accurate assessment of the existing situation. Managers often like to believe that the company is well known and liked in financial circles, when, in fact, such is not the case. Until there is an examination of how the company stands and what it can reasonably expect to do, any financial image program can be a gamble.

For some firms, this research will be conducted separately from its analysis of the general public attitude. The company wants to obtain a consensus among bankers, brokers, fund managers, and others in the financial world. Such a study is more than a nose-counting job and requires careful planning and skilled interviewing.

Amalgamations and promotion of securities are by no means the only, or even the major, objectives of financial public relations. Public relations certainly joins marketing, sales promotion, and advertising in creating sales, developing new markets, and building profits and increased volume. It is essential that the plans be directed toward the most desired targets.

The goodwill of suppliers is always desirable and can even be critical. In periods of shortages, materials are allocated to customers on the basis of their previous business and their relations with the supplier. There are occasions when special materials or services can become available to a limited number of customers or when favorable prices and terms can be granted to a few. These friendly relations are primarily established through personal contacts and reciprocal favors, but good publicity and advertising for the buyer will also influence the supplier. Everyone likes to be associated with success.

Community relations are usually local and not related to financial considerations, except where employees are concerned. There can be some cross-pollination when friendly neighbors may become customers or stockholders. This division of public relations will be discussed in Chapter 9.

One of PR's jobs may be to explain a bad situation. There was a time when most managements shunned any publicity when trouble occurred, whether it was a plant accident or a slump in earnings, but business now knows it is a mistake to fight or avoid the news media.

The explanation of unfavorable news should be as prompt as possible; it should really accompany the first announcement. The explanation should be complete and totally honest and should list the reasons for the trouble and how it is to be resolved. What must be avoided is any attempt to whitewash a manure pile—a difficult assignment indeed.

A Positive Response

During one of the periodic attacks on automobile safety, critics pointed out that thousands of cars had been recalled for possible replacement of parts. The industry countered that several series had been recalled, but only a small percentage needed a parts change. It was announced that this would be a continuing practice, and that the numbers and models to be recalled would be regularly announced. By making the recall an everyday matter, the edge was taken off criticism.

More recently, General Motors was charged with restricting competition and setting prices. GM's chairman, James Roche, submitted detailed, fact-filled reports and pointed out the fluctuations in share of market for different cars and companies. Most interesting of all, information on production costs was given. Of this campaign, *Time* said on November 1, 1968, that General Motors' statement "plainly showed the imprint of Chairman Roche, a one-time Cadillac publicist who has been laboring since he took command last November to brighten the company's image."

At about the same time, General Electric reported a drop in profits during a period when most corporations were showing gains. Chairman Fred J. Borch issued a statement that the company had invested tremendous sums in three new technical fields—nuclear power, computers, and aircraft engines. These newer divisions had not yet reached a point of profitability but were expected to make important contributions to earnings in coming years. In this way, investors were told that they sacrificed present earnings for the future growth and prosperity of the company.

Other problems have had an impact on the opinions of the financial community and demanded satisfactory explanation. Accidents to a series of new planes plagued one manufacturer. Some companies found merger partners so unsatisfactory that the corporate marriage was dissolved. Most unfortunate of all, a few firms have seen key executives flee to Brazil, leaving little in the way of assets and plenty in the way of trouble. Sometimes there is no immediate remedy, and the only possibility is a slow rebuilding of respect and confidence.

Communicating with the Financial World

Once objectives are satisfactorily agreed upon and targets selected, management will turn its attention to the *methods* of interesting the financial world. We have already discussed some annual and interim reports, publicity, advertising, direct mail, meetings, and appearances before security analysts. We have also referred to direct contacts by corporate officers with financial publishers and editors, security brokers, and investment and commercial bankers. It is worth our while to look at publicity and advertising more closely.

Unless the company provides interesting material to financial editors, there is little possibility that its accomplishments will be widely reported. Publishers and editors are busy people, and they are offered far more material than they can use. Their work is selecting and editing, as a rule. Occasionally a publication will seek out a story on some discovery or development, but usually the firm's PR department is way ahead of them and has released articles and illustrations.

Financial publicity should be an organized, continuing campaign, with specific personnel who are responsible for it. It should not be sporadic or accidental. It should be handled professionally, as publicity can be one of the most effective means of creating a favorable image at a relatively low cost.

It would be a mistake to think that only releases from large companies receive attention—smaller companies can and should make full use of publicity. Many achievements would not even be known unless releases were issued by the companies themselves. This can affect sales as well as financial recognition.

News Is the Essence

Unless a company has something interesting to report, the media won't use its releases. But what is news for one segment of the public is not necessarily interesting to another. Financial news is usually confined to a limited section of a few metropolitan daily newspapers and special publications. An announcement of new products may be important to the readers of an industrial magazine but will not run in most newspapers. Reports of people are usually of local interest only. The change of a plant manager or the civic work of an employee can be news in a small-town paper. If the corporation has stores or other properties around the country, the treatment of local news becomes part of the community program. It may be handled from headquarters or on the local level. Good local contact with news media is always desirable.

The principal news for financial publications deals with earnings or developments that will affect earnings. Readers look to this information with keen interest because it will affect their investments. Brokers and bankers check earnings reports as a basis for their own actions and recommendations to clients. In 1970 *Forbes* stated that a large credibility gap exists between corporations' statements of earnings and the beliefs of investment managers. The magazine said that sophisticated Wall Streeters consider earnings statements "almost useless as a basis for decision making," because "earnings" are largely a matter of interpretation.

In addition to statements of earnings or sales, financial news includes announcements of important new products or scientific developments. This does not ordinarily mean any new detergent or toothpaste, but if the detergent incorporates significant chemical advancements, or the toothpaste receives the approval of the American Dental Association, financial editors may be interested. Medical discoveries, new power sources, synthetic fabrics and their added uses, supersonic aircraft—these and hundreds of other products have been considered financial news.

All the business publications, such as *Fortune, Barron's, Business Week, The Wall Street Journal,* and *Forbes,* report on specific companies, as do the news weeklies on occasion. Some of the articles originate with the publishers, but most are prompted by company releases or contacts. Usually they are written or rewritten by the editorial staff and are not always favorable. If a company is in trouble, its problems may be analyzed and its management criticized. Sometimes the company has an opportunity to see the copy in advance, often it does not. In either case, it is helpful to have a good relationship with the publication. When commendatory material about the firm is published, reprints may usually be obtained for mailing to stockholders, brokers, and other public relations targets.

Another medium for publicity is the industrial, professional, and trade press. There are more than 2,000 magazines covering manufacturing, distribution, and marketing in every line of business and hundreds of technical and scientific journals. Some publications deal with only one phase of business, for example, *Sales Management, Distribution,* or *Product Design,* but most are directed to one industry. Most trade and industrial publications carry announcements of new products and personnel changes. Some magazines make only product announcements, a policy that can be helpful in industrial marketing.

In addition to news items, most business publications print case histories of firms in their particular industry or detailed articles on a company's operations. These are usually prepared in part, if not entirely, by the company, although they may result from invitations to the editors to visit plants and talk with management. In almost every case, the article is discussed ahead of time so that it can be prepared to suit both the company and the publisher.

What might be called a "piggyback recommendation" can be arranged in an article that links the firm's product or service to a successful operation elsewhere. An example would be the new use of a machine or process in a manufacturing plant. The reference is incidental to a general discussion, but the contribution of the machine is understood. Another example is the use of a packaging material (yours) to improve a marketing campaign (by another firm). When the 200-inch telescope was installed at Mt. Palomar, a problem of lubrication was solved by a new compound. Although the lubricant had relatively few other applications, Mobil Oil Company made good use of the development by publishing articles and news releases in which its name was linked with an unusual scientific achievement.

Modern space programs have given many firms an opportunity to ride on the vapor trails of the major contractors through publicity and advertising that told of their contributions to the overall system. Each successful flight had its satellite flights of publicity that helped the corporate images of large and small contractors.

Executives Use Direct Contacts

Securities analysts often invite corporation executives to address their meetings, and these opportunities can be solicited whenever the company has interesting data to disclose or is in the public eye. Executives of firms that are not well known and lack established contacts will be least likely to be invited. Financial editors usually report on these meetings, thus widening the effect of the firm's report.

The investing public assumes that a company will not seek or accept an invitation to address the analysts unless it has good news to report— the discovery of new resources, the announcement of new products, proposed acquisitions, or significant changes in the growth pattern. The aura surrounding such meetings has become so prominent that their advance announcement is sometimes reflected in a rise in the corporation's stock quotations.

Some analysts have complained that corporation presentations can be more show than substance. Some are principally propaganda, dressed up with motion pictures or other devices. There is no objection to entertainment if it tells a worthwhile story, but there must be meaningful information and answers to pertinent questions.

In addition to formal meetings, it is important that the corporation officials develop less formal contacts with securities analysts, brokerage company managers, editors and publishers of financial news media, and investment and commercial bankers. This can be done by inviting one person or a small group to visit a new facility, have lunch with two or three of the company's executives, and discuss the current situation and prospective developments.

When friendly relations have been established with key men in the financial community, they can be maintained through further meetings, telephone contact, or correspondence. When the corporation needs attention and help, it is much easier to reach men who know and respect the management.

The support of an active brokerage house has the effect of the pebble in the pool—the ripples continue to spread in constantly widening circles. Direct recommendations may be made to individual or institutional investors. Some of the large firms publish a list of recommended securities and issue comments and recommendations to their customers' men every day. Most have periodic bulletins and regular market summaries in which action on specific stocks is suggested. These are sent to all the firm's clients and are available to prospective investors.

Contact with publishers or editors may not materially change the direction of their articles, but their knowledge of the company may foster an explanation or avoid a misunderstanding. When relations with a publication are cordial, it is much easier to present the corporation's side of the situation. This presentation is partly the responsibility of the public relations department, but it should be supported by senior management contacts.

Brokers, bankers, and investors look to information services for data on corporations and for recommendations. Dozens of services are available; some cover a large number of stocks and others concentrate on specific groups. Some are based on fundamental information; others use technical charts to forecast the market direction. Leading services are regularly quoted in financial publications. Usually, all the services want from management is accurate and complete information.

Brokerage firms conduct forums or seminars for the education of clients and prospects. Specific stocks are discussed at these meetings, and it is reasonable to expect that brokers will recommend stocks they know well and regard highly.

Institutional Advertising Increases

Advertising aimed at creating or enhancing a favorable corporate image rather than attracting customers for products or services has come into wider use. Most of these campaigns appear in business or financial publications, but there is some use of general magazines and television for corporate advertising.

The dollar return from any advertising is difficult to calculate; bench marks for financial advertising include the price of securities, a growing or declining number of shareholders, the rate of investments by funds, results of recruiting campaigns, and recognition by financial news media. Institutional advertising is usually a greater reflection of top management than is consumer advertising, and when it is well done, it shows the direct results of good management planning and attention.

In an advertisement, a corporation can make statements exactly as it wishes them to be heard or read. There is always a possibility that publicity releases will be curtailed, revised, or not used at all; this does not happen to advertising copy. Advertising can be run whenever management wants to make an announcement, extend a tender offer, or answer criticism. It is usually easier to reach the desired audience through public advertising than by mail when an urgent message is essential.

Institutional advertisers have one problem that does not face some consumer advertisers—there is usually no existing interest in what is being advertised. While most readers are unconcerned about the doings of a tubing manufacturer or a fish cannery, their attention is caught by advertisements for such personal needs as cars, apparel, or foods.

This makes it necessary for financial advertising to create interest *first* and then get its message across. This can be achieved through good advertising techniques, plus information that can be made of interest to the reader. Some corporate advertisements can have a broader interest than others. Their use depends on the purpose of the campaign, the audience to which it is aimed, and the appeals that are logical for this particular corporation to use.

There is a trend toward separating corporate advertising from consumer campaigns; companies often use different agencies or company departments. The financial program is usually handled by public relations. Separate budgets are set up, with corporation programs paid for and controlled by a financial officer, not the marketing department.

The appeals of this advertising follow the objectives of the image program and should be focused on matters of especial interest to investors and other members of the financial community. These are most likely to be major changes, with or without a name change, the announcement of a merger or acquisition, reports of sales growth and profits, activities abroad, or the success of particular equipment or services. Advertising may also stress the search for acquisition candidates, describe the corporation's present activities, announce significant new products, and discuss the philosophy of management. Important markets, current news, and entertainment activities all may be vital aspects of advertising appeals. Or advertising may be based on the company's customers. It may celebrate its history or its anniversary or describe corporate activities in the community. It is obvious that these arbitrary classifications may be overlapping, and that some advertisements will use more than one appeal. There are also advertisements that are specific in their message, directed to limited sectors of the financial world, such as announcements of the sale of new security issues, advertising by mutual funds, and advertisements urging shareholders to act one way or the other on outstanding tender offers.

In addition to the long-range objectives of the financial PR program, there may be short-term campaigns. Most firms have problems and opportunities arising from their activities that can affect both the business and the corporate image. There may be plans for a factory in a new community that will bring added payrolls but may not be welcomed because of the location. It becomes important to convince the community that benefits outweigh the objections.

9

Community, Industry, and Employee Relations

A corporation's image in its own community is of growing concern to management. This concern applies not only to the headquarters city but also to every plant, warehouse, office, or store that carries the company name. Consideration should start with the location of office buildings, service stations, or branches and with the appearance of the firm's properties. For most companies, location and building design are already fixed, but their maintenance and identification can always be improved.

Staffing the work force is no longer just a matter of hiring the necessary number of workers for available jobs. It is a sensitive matter of helping the community and meeting the requirements of the federal and state governments as well as operating the business.

If the corporation has retail or service outlets, all its policies of doing business, the appearance and manners of employees, and the products or services it offers become part of its image in the community.

Involvement in the civic, political, and charitable activities of each community must also be considered. Special corporate events, changes in policy or key personnel, and other news may be of interest to the firm's neighbors.

Responsibility for each phase of the corporation's activities should be made clear in the organization chart and job assignments for every area. Are the policies to be set locally or at headquarters? Which functions can be handled by which people, and to whom do they look for approval?

Management and staff personnel who are concerned with the corporate image should work as closely as possible with people in the field and with the marketing and industrial relations departments. When actions or announcements that affect the firm's relations in the community are made, personnel should understand the limits of authority and methods of handling emergencies.

Social Responsibility

Industry has finally begun to recognize its social responsibility. This is not, by any means, simply a matter of doing good for others. The welfare and life of a corporation, at least in a community, will depend more and more on this social consciousness. In an extreme case, its continued existence could be threatened.

In 1958, Dr. Laurence M. Gould, then president of Carleton College, included this statement in one of his addresses:

> But somehow I do not believe the greatest threat to our future is from bombs or guided missiles. I don't think our civilization will die that way. I think it will die when we no longer care—when the spiritual forces that make us wish to be right and noble die in the hearts of men. Arnold Toynbee has pointed out that 19 of 21 notable civilizations have died from within and not by conquest from without. There were no bands playing and no flags waving when these civilizations decayed; it happened slowly, in the quiet and the dark when no one was aware.

In industry's analysis of its problems and responsibilities in the community, it is clearly brought out that prosperity and so-called high employment are not enough, because they do not touch the hard-core poor. When minority groups set up businesses of their own, it becomes apparent that there are relatively few experienced managers and that a certain percentage of ghetto residents have never had the opportunity to form good work habits. This situation is further reflected in the growing number of people on relief rolls although industry seeks an ever increasing number of workers.

Training programs in industry have been emphasized; to some extent, they are intended to replace government programs. They always present the same problems, however they are administrated, but are generally regarded as essential. Organized labor has expressed resentment about special favors given minority workers, such as pay during training programs, automatic seniority, and advancement before merit is fully demonstrated.

All this adds up to the fact that management now finds its employment policies as vital and as troublesome as other major functions.

Programs for hiring formerly unacceptable men and training unskilled workers have been announced and widely publicized by companies in Detroit, Minneapolis, and other cities. It is evident that progress will be slower than desired, but both industry and government are becoming committed to these campaigns.

In Pittsburgh, PPG Industries organized a ten-week pre-employment and job counseling program for minority-group women who had not been able to get secretarial jobs after leaving high school. Professional teachers set up a curriculum that included language and mathematics as well as vocational skills. The girls were trained under simulated office conditions. The company reports good results and plans to expand the program as well as offer new job opportunities in PPG plants.

Life insurance companies' interests in ghetto problems have been consistent and are expressed in this message from The Equitable Life Assurance Society:

> If you're concerned with the times we live in, so are we at Equitable. With people at odds, cities and towns in decay, there's a lot to be done to make life more livable. Equitable is trying to help. By investing millions to rebuild slums, provide decent housing, create new jobs. By encouraging Americans everywhere to support the Urban Coalition— to give a hand where it's needed.

After 18 months of active participation by the Institute of Life Insurance and investment of approximately one billion dollars by its members, the Institute stated that an additional billion was to be committed. In a public announcement, response and help from others were asked because:

A lot that is said about urban problems is pure myth.

For example, it might seem very gratifying to businessmen if all they had to do was apply some corporate mind and money to make the cities bloom overnight again. Or, alternatively, if they could simply hang a "For Government Only" sign on the subject and walk away from all responsibility. We in the life insurance business found from experience that neither response is valid.

In 1969, the National Alliance of Businessmen was pledged to hire 500,000 hard-core workers by mid-1971. The NAB designated 125 cities in which disadvantaged workers should be hired even if they lacked ordinary qualifications. Corporations pledged themselves to employ specific numbers of these disadvantaged workers. At a later date, other cities will become qualified for the NAB campaign. It should be pointed out that effective results from the program depend on local management rather than on home office direction.

Urban Orientation holds seminars and distributes materials to educate local, middle-management groups in the employment and training of disadvantaged people. A major subject is the need to change the point of view of supervisors who, in many cases, do not appreciate or understand the needs of their new trainees.

In every part of the country, there are groups and organizations challenging individual firms to take part in employment and other social problems. The response of these companies is becoming a significant part of a favorable or adverse image.

A brief roundup in *The Wall Street Journal's* "Labor Letter" of October 21, 1969, was headed "Do-Good Projects Occupy More Time of the Nation's Top Executives." The article elaborated as follows:

Time, Inc.'s chairman Andrew Heiskell spends over 20 percent of his time working for such organizations as the Urban Coalition. Ampex Corporation's President William Roberts, who serves as chairman of the pollution-fighting San Francisco Bay Area Council, contends that today's business leaders can't afford to be "narrow-gauged." A Transamerica Corporation veep notes that do-good demands on the conglomerate "have increased tremendously as we've become better known."

Most executives say outside activities haven't hurt their regular work but simply cut into leisure time. Commonwealth Edison President Thomas Ayers, who devotes 10 to 15 hours weekly to civic projects in Chicago, abandons an evening round of golf. At Marcor Inc., former Chairman Robert Brooker said, "We regard participation in civic work as part of the self-development of an executive."

Employee Attitudes

Another aspect of a company's image is its relations with its own employees. Some corporations run year after year with no labor problems and maintain a high rate of production; others are in constant turmoil that is expressed in wildcat strikes, slowdowns, and low productivity. It is not expected that public relations will make any great difference in such a situation; on the contrary, the company's labor troubles can blemish its general reputation.

Plant closings or moves to another area either can cause trouble or can be handled so well that trouble is avoided. This, again, is not primarily dependent on public relations so much as it is on the company's attitude and policies, but here PR can really help.

Probably the most traumatic situation arises when the company makes a public announcement that it will close or move a plant, without first consulting with the employees. This would seem so obvious a mistake that no firm would commit the error, but some have. If employees are first told about the firm's plans for transfers to another plant or efforts to arrange local jobs, there can be a feeling of mutual cooperation. The community does not become so upset at the loss of the corporate payroll and the problems that separation will cause. The PR department can talk with the local news media and explain the reasons behind the company's plans and its program to ease the employees' problems by severance pay, transfers, or arrangements for other employment.

A threatened strike can cause a loss of business to a company or an industry, even if the strike never takes place. When it appears that a strike may hit the steel industry, customers start looking for other sources. They import steel or consider the use of other materials. When it is announced that a union plans to strike one of the automobile companies, prospective car buyers look elsewhere for their new models. Too often, this announcement comes from the union rather than the company, and the firm has little opportunity to control the adverse publicity. What *is* sometimes possible is creation of public support for a reasonable settlement.

In a community and, to some extent, in the corporation itself, its image will be affected by the personal expressions of employees. This is one more instance where person-to-person recommendations or denouncements are stronger than mass communications. There must be a fundamental feeling of satisfaction in the employees to produce a happy relationship; this is not something that can be created by edict.

It is, however, something that can be improved by education, by giving employees information about their own company—its products, policies, accomplishments, and plans. This gives people pride in the company and something of interest to tell their friends. People like to be regarded as authorities and to have inside information. There is real satisfaction in making a recommendation that is accepted, particularly if the person receiving it is pleased with the result.

Employees do not think about their company as a whole. They will discuss it as a good or bad place to work; they will report on the results of its profit-sharing plan and whether the company stock is a good investment, or they will talk about the firm's products and services or new projects that are being started.

The more accurately and completely this information is supplied by management, the better it will reflect what management wants the company to represent. As has been explained, this can be done through house organs, bulletins, meetings, and all the other lines of communication that exist in the organization.

As business becomes more closely involved in community affairs and urban problems, the policies and practices of each corporation will be discussed even more often by its employees and customers as well as its industry neighbors. All in all, workers can help significantly to change or project the image. A large national firm can have hundreds of thousands of spokesmen—every company has a field force in its community. This fact is recognized by firms that have well-organized communications.

Employees can attract new investors by their comments on the firm's progress, new products, or profit expectations. Companies have stock ownership plans for employees, and any comment on the success of these programs interests other people.

Among the activities of employees in local plants or offices that are usually governed by corporate policy are donations to charities and participation in charity drives, civic enterprises, and political organizations.

Most firms set up guidelines for handling news during emergencies and for releasing stories and pictures that are of interest to the community.

One area in which large corporations and industry groups have been singularly ineffective is their public relations during labor controversies. The unions have usually been quicker to get their story before the public and they have been more persuasive. Because politics enters strongly into labor relations, and federal administrations have often supported labor, companies have been pushed into industrywide bargaining, combinations of unions at one conference table, and other concessions. Most firms have waited until union demands are on record before making any statement about negotiations and, therefore, have not been effective in presenting their arguments.

Good Relations Attract Customers

One of the results of good community relations, education of employees, and good communication is that new customers are attracted and present ones retained. This is particularly true of firms with retail outlets and consumer products or services, but such relations can also affect the acceptance of industrial materials. In many lines of business, offerings are so similar and competition so keen that increased volume and profit may substantially depend on the public's feelings about an institution.

Banks usually offer the same interest rates on savings and approximately the same privileges for checking accounts. This means that people will select a particular bank for such peripheral reasons as its convenient location, its favorable personality, or unusual service. Banks have largely discarded their former austerity. Executives are approachable, and principal officers are in close contact with the public. Some banks serve coffee in cold weather or dress their cashiers in attractive uniforms, and most of them have employees on hand to supply information or needed forms.

Bankers are regularly concerned with community affairs and civic developments and publicize their participation whenever possible. Bank advertising seldom has its former extreme dignity; now television commercials offer special overdraft accounts and free checking with minimum balances, and newspaper and outdoor advertising often employ cartoons and other devices to gain attention and a friendly response.

Department and chain stores feature special events—not only Santa Claus at Christmas but holiday parades, Easter floral exhibits, and back-to-school events. Shopping centers are the scene of auto shows, pet parades, or the circus. Every effort is made to give the institution a distinct personality. The impression may be one of high fashion, thrift, or unusual services, depending on the image sought.

A growing corporate concern is customer complaints. More firms are making an effort to learn from salesmen, dealers, and through direct calls or letters whether customer reactions are good or bad. Some firms have set up special departments to handle customer relations. Such arrangements can be effective only if management gets accurate reports from the marketing organization. All the value of advertising, publicity, and good management can be lost if a customer feels that a legitimate complaint is not properly handled.

Industrial firms are now paying more attention to customer relations out of a conviction that good service is a profitable policy. Billing methods are examined to make sure both that no time is being lost in billing and collection and that there are fewer misunderstandings on the part of customers. Delivery systems are studied, credit policies reviewed.

Consumer advisers at all levels of government, the National Product Safety Commission, and the Federal Trade Commission have all expressed growing concern about the inability of manufacturers and dealers to handle customer complaints promptly and satisfactorily. Among the charges brought against business are failure to respond to questions or complaints, the general practice of "passing the buck," faulty products, lack of available service for mechanical products, and misdeliveries. If manufacturers reply that only a tiny percentage of customers are unsatisfied, the agencies contend that only the tip of the iceberg is seen and the dissatisfaction is much deeper than it appears.

One policy that seems to have improved customer relations is that some manufacturers, not the dealer, now accept responsibility for warranties. Retailers and producers have generally accused each other of unsatisfactory handling of customers. Where the maker takes immediate action on all complaints, there is no argument.

It is also charged that, in many companies, no responsible executive hears or reads complaints; they are handled by a separate department that may be principally concerned with saving money. The best solution seems to be direct communication with responsible people and a policy of customer satisfaction. Unsatisfactory handling of complaints not only hurts an image but can result in more government interference.

Firms Become Good Neighbors

Campaigns to gain the favor of the public are standard practice for a number of corporations. For the last 40 years, Standard Oil of California has been identified with good music programs for schools in its areas. In the beginning programs were broadcast by radio for classroom listening; more recently, live concerts have been staged for both schools and the public.

Standard Oil has also made scenic motion pictures available for group and club meetings through its staff organization. Mobil Oil provided equipment for student-driver tests in public schools without cost. Auto firms have made cars available for student drivers. Many firms schedule regular visits by school groups to plants where foods or beverages are prepared. Some industrial firms also invite school or other special-interest groups.

Factory or store openings can be the occasion for inviting employees and their families as well as representatives of the community. The event may be celebrated with appropriate souvenirs and literature as well as refreshments. Stores and other service units have a more commercial reason for opening events; they want everyone to see their merchandise and become customers.

Exhibits at fairs or shows are usually designed to promote the corporate image. Some outstanding ones have become favorites of fair visitors. Animation, special motion pictures, and other special effects make production of these exhibits involved and expensive; to justify such complexity, they should make a strong and favorable impression.

An interesting campaign to improve the image of business in general and of specific corporations is the Junior Achievement program. This is a national organization in which high school students form business companies, for which they raise capital and produce and market goods or services. These companies are operated according to standard practices, scaled down to size. The students issue stock, keep accounts and issue reports, pay rent and interest, and eventually try to liquidate their corporations profitably.

Each JA firm is sponsored by an established business, although the activities of each may be quite different. The support of one large corporation was expressed in the following advertisement, signed by Russell De-Young, chairman of the Goodyear Tire & Rubber Company.

Your Daughter the President.

She's 16 years old (give or take a year). She's from any background. She's of any race, any religion. Any nationality.

And she's president of a corporation. A very, very small one, but a corporation none the less.

And it's all made possible through Junior Achievement.

An organization that feels kids just shouldn't kid around about their future. So, for the past 50 years, Junior Achievement has been teaching high school boys and girls the value and workings of free enterprise, through a unique economics program. . . .

We can't think of a better start for teenagers who want to enter the business world after college. And we can't think of a better time, during JA's 50th anniversary, to show our continued support.

Some corporations hold a tight rein on PR activities, preferring to have them carried out under home-office direction by special staff members. Other firms have extended PR authority throughout the organization, encouraging all employees to talk about the company before community groups or to take part in local activities that call attention to the firm.

Contributions may be controlled by company policy, but in plant and store communities these donations are made by the local manager. His participation in charity or civic campaigns usually depends on available time and personal inclinations.

The Role of Company Properties

The location, size, and design of a corporation's headquarters building will usually be decided by considerations other than its effect on the company's image, but there is no doubt that once built, the structure becomes an important part of that image. Certainly a bank or insurance company wants its building to be regarded favorably by present and potential customers; a steel or aluminum manufacturer may have no local recognition other than that of its downtown headquarters.

It is possible that a new building can be used, at least locally, to spark a general change in the identity of a corporation. Transfer from an old structure or outdated location to an impressive new headquarters may be made to attract favorable attention. If this move coincides with adoption of a new name or symbol, the benefits can be broader, even attracting regional or national attention.

Granting that the image will not be the determining factor in building plans, there are still considerations for management. Some corporations have been praised for locating in undeveloped sections of the city or participating in broad plans for improvement of a downtown area. Pittsburgh's "golden triangle," the former produce section of San Francisco, downtown Philadelphia and Boston, and redevelopment plans for Bunker Hill in Los Angeles are examples.

There have been a number of buildings located so as to provide an island of landscaped space in a crowded city and thus earn the appreciation of natives and visitors. Usually this distinction is linked to good architecture and sound use of space; all elements combine for a favorable impression. Rockefeller Center set an example that has been followed by the Crown Zellerbach building in San Francisco and a number of distinctive structures in Southern California.

In a number of cities, there has been an option between locating the headquarters downtown, on the periphery of the city, or in the suburbs. Crowded and rundown central areas have been abandoned by many corporations that have located where conditions are more pleasant and the time and effort required to go to and from work are substantially reduced. Business and industrial parks a good many miles from city centers have attracted office staffs as well as production workers.

There can be strong public feeling about the specific location and design of a new building. This can result in protests against high-rise structures that block a view or create congestion. San Francisco's downtown building boom has the blessing of local officials and developers, but the resentment of many residents and visitors. In four years, 17 high-rise office buildings and at least a dozen hotels and other highly visible structures have changed the skyline of that city. Allan Temco, a writer for architectural reviews, says of the new skyline,

> Esthetically, there is no question that inadequate attention is being given to the massiveness of some of these buildings in San Francisco. They shut off the sunlight, they cause the hills to lose their impact, and they interfere with the view of the bay.

His ideas are supported by Theodore Osmundsen, president of the American Society of Landscape Architects, who condemns the city's "Manhattanization" in these words:

Some think that's wonderful, but I think it's absolutely outrageous. San Francisco has unique landscape features. To clog it with buildings, each cutting off the view of the other, would destroy everything people want in San Francisco.

Development or Pollution?

San Francisco can be used as a further example, because in that area there are plans and problems that will face other communities. There is a long-range battle about development of lands around and under San Francisco Bay. The water area has already shrunk nearly 40 percent, and conservationists are alarmed about further water and air pollution, urban crowding, and loss of natural wild life. Important firms and individuals are seeking to develop large areas of tide flats for industrial and residential use. Under construction is one of the first major rapid transit systems to be built in recent years.

How the corporate owner of land carries out its development is vital to its relations with the community. There is no doubt that only through development can rising costs and taxes be offset. Opposing forces will give the management no peace, and it will take wise judgment to make the best decisions.

Factories, warehouses, and other buildings outside the city can also have an effect on the feelings of neighbors. It has been demonstrated that factories need not be eyesores by the effective design of many new industrial plants and the interesting use of new materials and construction methods.

Different and more difficult problems are involved in the face-lifting of an old building. The original design may permit only a limited change, both inside and out. Only a new structure makes possible a total program. Here the corporation should look years into the future and design without fads or gimmicks that will date their headquarters.

An Architectural Point of View

Corporate identity as expressed in architecture and urban design is discussed by Marc Goldstein, associate partner in Skidmore, Owings & Merrill:

Broadly speaking, there are three modes of corporate identification from an architectural point of view.

The first of course is quite simply "the sign." This is by far the most common method employed. The guiding principle seems to be the bigger the better. Almost invariably these large signs make a mockery of the buildings which are forced to support them. Any attention which has been paid to form and proportion in the evolution of the design of the building is ludicrously negated by the sign. However, the custom persists despite the fact that the public is becoming impatient with this kind of egoism, as is evidenced by sign ordinances increasingly appearing all over the country.

The second method of achieving corporate identity is to allow the building itself to become a sign. That is, the building becomes so distinctive that a sign is clearly superfluous. When this technique is employed by a superbly gifted architect, the results can be glorious, as in the case of the Larkin Building built by Frank Lloyd Wright in 1904 or the C.B.S. Building built by Eero Saarinen in 1967. Unfortunately, there are not that many superbly gifted architects around. Most frequently, this approach to the problem leads to an embarrassing kind of architectural acrobatics. As more and more of these buildings are built, our cities take on the characteristics of an urban zoo—each building calling out for attention, the whole cacophony finally becoming something of a bore.

Happily, there is a third way in which a corporation can identify itself. It may do so by seeing the creation of a building or group of buildings as an opportunity to enhance its immediate surroundings rather than overwhelm them. By seeking to contribute to the urban scene rather than simply to blow its own horn, a corporation will, in my view, achieve the best kind of image.

The classic example is Rockefeller Center, the success of which is due as much to the spaces between the buildings as the buildings themselves. Other examples would include the Seagram Building and Chase Manhattan Building, whose plazas were among the first privately developed public places in America. Another would be the Ford Foundation Building, with its marvelous garden creating a kind of public living room on 42nd Street.

Admittedly, these are dramatic examples, but they serve to make a point. The strongest image is not necessarily "visual"—it may be psychological, a response to the provision of amenities, to good neighborliness. Amenities may take many forms—plazas, arcades, patios, gardens, trees, works of art, or simply places to sit. Size is not the issue. The right tree in the right place in front of a small building can be as meaningful as a large open space in front of a large building. In short, a strong public image is best achieved simply by serving the public.

Problems Explained

There are times when a corporation can incur, or be threatened with, the ill will of a community. Avoidance of such developments depends on careful cooperation between local groups and management. To avoid controversy with special groups, such as conservationists, a corporation should explain long-range programs that might otherwise be misunderstood.

An example of the need for such public explanation is modern tree farming, or reforestation, as practiced by lumber companies. These firms have been accused of exploiting natural resources, of destroying forests that should have been protected by government, of employing wasteful methods.

Growth of trees for future selective cutting, and utilization of every part of the tree in one product or another, are practiced by the large wood-products firms to perpetuate their business and improve their profits. Such policies are not established primarily to offset criticism, but they have proved effective in influencing public and government opinion. The firms in this field keep their story before people through publicity, advertising, and motion pictures as an essential theme in the public relations programs.

One of the most vigorous campaigns of the 1960s was the steel industry's protest against growing imports. This was directed at Congress, with the establishment of import quotas or higher tariffs as the goal. At the same time, a broad program to the public urged voters to influence their representatives in favor of the domestic industry. In late 1968, foreign producers offered to set voluntary quotas on shipments to the United States, hoping to prevent more stringent controls.

Industrywide Campaigns

There are hundreds of industry and trade associations in every part of the country; some are national and others local or regional. Each county has its medical and dental groups, its organizations of lawyers, architects, and other professionals. One function of each association, sometimes the most important, is the protection of the image of its business or profession.

Trouble seems to be the reason that most industries get together on public relations. When there are organized criticism and opposition, members of the business become more willing to spend time and money for protection of their interests.

One decision facing management in its assessment of industry campaigns is the extent to which time and money should be contributed to the general program rather than to the firm's own promotion. The decision will be different for each industry and every corporation, and will depend on the extent and success of cooperative campaigns and the personal interests of the firm's executives. Other factors will be the time available for association work, the needs of the industry, the corporation's place in the total picture, and the availability of capable participants.

Railroads are an industry in which the principal PR effort is made by one organization, the Association of American Railroads. The campaign is directed to the public as well as to shippers. Prime-time television commercials have been used to describe new railroad practices, such as computer control and piggyback container cars. The campaign is evidently designed to create goodwill for the railroads as well as to promote freight business.

Some railroads have tried to change public opinion of their passenger service and new high-speed trains have been installed, but most give the impression that they would like to abandon all of their passenger trains. Most railroad promotion is for freight traffic, for which railroads compete with motor transport and air cargo.

The American Trucking Association conducts most of the campaigns for motor transport and for many years has maintained an organization of public relations representatives throughout the country. The campaigns are directed against special taxes on trucks and charges of damage to highways and are in favor of larger trailers and less regulation. Public interest and support are solicited on the basis that most localities would not have freight service without trucks. Contact with legislators and government agencies is a major part of the program.

The Redwood Association bands together producers of redwood lumber and products in defense of the industry's logging practices as well as for promotion to customers. There has been vigorous public activity to preserve certain redwood forests as state or national parks, and well-organized appeals to the public and to legislators have been made. The association seeks to explain its policies and activities through publication advertising, motion pictures, and all available public relations media.

The automobile industry may have to consider whether it wants to respond as an industry to the growing attacks on it. It has been under fire for not moving fast enough with safety precautions and equipment, with delaying antipollution devices, and failure to provide adequate service under factory warranties. Each of these campaigns is at least a short-term problem for manufacturers and may become a long-range controversy, a threat to the industry image, and a challenge to management.

Automobile insurance is another field in which demands for action may cause acute image problems. The business is challenged to revise fundamental policies and to adopt a plan for payments to all persons involved in accidents, regardless of liability. The legal profession, understandably, looks at this plan without enthusiasm and denies the claims of its advocates.

Product Troubles Create Havoc

Troubles with products can cause serious business loss. Several years ago, cranberry growers lost much of their holiday business when their fruit was said to be carrying poisonous insecticide. Growers countered by inducing public figures to eat cranberries, and over a period of time business was restored. Another crisis was caused by a number of deaths attributed to botulism from canned tuna. For six months, there was virtually no sale for tuna in many areas; again, time smoothed the situation.

A large part of the agricultural-chemicals industry has been under fire about the effects of insecticide residues on fruits and vegetables and their contribution to water pollution. The cigarette business is not only facing restrictions on advertising but also a strong campaign by national health organizations and government officials as well. The drug industry has been charged with maintaining high prices and profits at the expense of the sick and with selling medications that are ineffective or even dangerous.

In cases where illness or death is involved, there is a big question of whether to publicly deny and challenge the accusations or wait quietly for the storm to subside. There is always a possibility that direct and vigorous denial will simply call further attention to the accusations.

Most corporations are involved in these problems only as members of an industry, although specific corporations *have* been directly charged. Each firm should have an established plan for meeting such emergencies, with the chain of command set up, authority designated for decisions, and assignments made for the preparation of rebuttals.

10

Organization, Budgeting, and Measuring the Results

IN most corporations, proposals and plans for a new image program will be considered by a senior management committee and may be assigned to a special committee for execution and control. The committee system establishes a consensus on the proposals and spreads the responsibility for decisions, as it does in other corporate operations.

The standing or special committee assigned to the image program will supervise staff departments and veto or confirm the offerings of consultants, designers, or other outside organizations. Details of the campaign, creation of materials, and communications with target audiences will usually be the work of a public relations department together with outside assistance.

Most corporations have assigned their corporate advertising to the same agency that handles their product campaigns, but those who want a separate program seek an agency that is known for institutional advertising. Such an arrangement is often satisfactory to the agencies, as organizations working principally on hard-hitting product campaigns may not be set up for financial public relations programs.

There are now more special agencies that concentrate on financial public relations, and they are being employed by a wider number of corporations. This is largely due to the stricter requirements for disclosure of information and to the rapidly growing interest in the financial community. These agencies are used in the event of mergers, tenders, and proxy battles.

Within the company, the general campaign of financial PR is usually handled by the firm's public relations department under the direction and control of a financial officer or the chief executive.

The demand in 1969 created a shortage of men skilled in both public relations and financial matters. One employment agency characterized the desired man as "a systems engineer with Wall Street experience who writes like Shakespeare." Major PR firms report shortages of specialized personnel and say that product publicity men are seldom qualified for financial programs.

A study by the Securities and Exchange Commission found that corporate publicity can have a powerful effect on stock prices, and there is no question that active corporations have used every possible means of taking their stories to the public.

Preparation Is Shared

Financial information for the annual and interim reports is necessarily produced by the corporation and its auditors, but the rest of the material is strictly public relations. Decisions on size, style, and contents are usually at the executive level but are developed from recommendations of the staff. Some companies use their advertising or public relations agencies to help prepare the annual report.

Even more involved in creating these reports are the design organizations that specialize in symbols, format and illustrations for corporate literature, and institutional advertising layouts and logotypes. There are about a dozen nationally known designers who have created most of the outstanding new programs and are responsible for the appearance of many reports. In addition, there are regional organizations, advertising, and PR agencies that also produce this type of material.

When a new image program has been successfully created by a design firm, the same firm is usually assigned further work—reports, packages, and other means of identification. Some corporations have divided their assignments, using one designer for the major trademark or symbol program and another for the annual report or their packages.

Most of the designers recommend creation of a complete program, but some are willing to accept a single assignment in order to get started working with the corporation. One of the national groups advocates trial assignments, so that management can evaluate the ability of the designers.

Assuming that the corporation is sincerely committed to a new image, it is considered sounder practice to lay out the whole program, including the complete system of identifications, for all channels of communications. This should include whatever research is to be done and should precede the actual design of materials. This makes it possible to consider whatever is submitted against the entire program. Some firms have changed their designer at this point, but at least the concept of a complete program was not undone.

Lippincott & Margulies, Inc., a creator of major programs, strongly supports the principle of a complete program. In one of its reports, L&M says:

In the past, companies have employed a piecemeal approach when attempting to shore up signs of weakness. Without any overall plan, they tried to do the job without relating efforts in one or several of these areas:

- Special corporate advertising
- Strong brand advertising
- New division advertising
- Changing public relations agencies
- A corporate identity program
- Extra promotion drives
- More product publicity
- New marketing strategy
- Redesigned packaging
- Changing of symbol

Now a broader perspective calls for combining efforts in all these areas, using them as building blocks in a total communications program. This not only multiplies their effectiveness and greatly increases their efficiency, but it provides the consistency and strength of overall impression that is essential for successful communication in today's ever more crowded and competitive marketplace.

The head of an organization specializing in visual communications, Robert Miles Runyan, has this opinion:

Every corporation that seeks to introduce a new image or improve an existing identity should use outside counsel and services for its communications, just as it would use auditors, attorneys, and business consultants for other specific needs.

Runyan feels that it is important to have one organization control and coordinate all aspects of visual communications, although others may be selected for specific assignments. He feels it is critical to bring in counsel before objectives are set and to base program decisions on research. When the program is established on a sound basis of surveys and resulting targets, it should be done completely. If it is done part at one time, part at another, it will not be impressive.

Good Public Relations Is Vital

Primary responsibility for public relations falls on the chief executive in almost every corporation and, to some extent, the image of the company is a reflection of this man. Once policy and motivation have been established, the top man must have the assistance of a competent public relations department. The selection of a man to head this department can materially affect the program.

There is a strong trend toward elevating the rank of the public relations manager. He should be at an equal level with the department and division heads and have authority enough for contacts with principal media. In an increasing number of firms, the public relations department is headed by a vice-president or an assistant to the president. In most companies, he is directly responsible to the chief executive.

In addition to creating or directing effective material, the PR head must be able to get along well with others in the firm and with outside contacts. In many companies, he needs either a sound knowledge of financial operations or such a specialist in his department.

Product advertising is not often handled by the PR department, but institutional advertising usually is. Corporate advertising may be directed by a financial officer through the PR staff and outside agencies.

The successive steps in the evaluation of an existing image, the formulation of objectives for a new one, and determination of methods by which the program is to be promoted will usually be divided among internal departments of the company and outside agencies or consultants. Some aspects of the program are highly specialized and should be handled by the most competent people available.

The Place of Outside Organizations

Among the outside organizations that may logically be used are opinion researchers, advertising agencies, public relations agencies, financial public relations counselors, designers, decorators, architects, film producers, and management consultants.

The decisions to employ outsiders to supplement internal departments or take over complete assignments will depend on such factors as the size of the corporation, the complexity of the new program, the time element, and the availability of capable personnel within the company. As in other corporate operations, there is a growing use of experienced outside specialists for certain parts of an image program.

It is important to know that an outside organization does specialize successfully, and to avoid any group that is not fully qualified for a specific assignment, no matter how helpful it may be in other work. There is a natural tendency for agencies or consultants already employed by the firm to reach for as many assignments as possible. The advertising agency may wish to conduct research or have its art department design new symbols. The public relations department may feel that it should undertake any new program of financial PR. With the best of intentions, these groups may not have the capability or experience for what may be difficult assignments. Time will be lost while they learn, or the entire campaign can go wrong if managed by incompetent people.

This does not mean that the departments of a corporation should not be involved in a new image program. It is essential for them to have an important part and handle all functions for which they are well qualified. Before a new program is started, every department and every division should be consulted, both to check on proposed changes and to speed communications.

Agencies and consultants should be selected by the senior officer (preferably the chief executive) who is directing the image program. He will have the guidance of staff personnel and make his selections from their recommendations. In any carefully prepared program, there will be lengthy preparation for key moves.

The choice of an opinion research firm to evaluate the existing image will depend on what information is wanted from the survey. If all that is needed is a check on recognition of the name or symbols or knowledge of the firm's products, any nose-counting organization can do this job. One of the few critical factors could be the selection of respondents to be sure that a field representing the desired target is surveyed.

When it is important to know what certain specific people really think of the corporation, there must be more intensive research. As outlined earlier, this calls for skilled interviewers, careful preparation of the questionnaire, and accurate evaluation of returns. The interviewer will seldom ask a direct question about the sponsoring corporation. A more usual technique is to ask the interviewee to select one among several companies and to then probe for the reasons this one is favored over the others.

The selection of outside organizations is much the same for designers, advertising or public relations agencies, or financial consultants. The major consideration is always how well the outside firm fits the specific needs of the particular client. This is more important than general reputation or record. For example, size must be considered. Is the design firm or agency of appropriate size? If there is need for service in various parts of the country or the world, can this be obtained? Is the staff varied enough to provide all necessary services? On the other hand, there is no point in giving a small assignment to a large organization, where it will not be an important account, nor is it usually wise to expect a small group to handle a growing and demanding client.

And what about experience? Are there people in the agency who understand the business of the corporation? For what classifications of industry has the organization worked? Does it have specialized knowledge or experience if this is needed by the client?

It is also essential to know who will work on the account. There is no value in meeting the president or chief designers if they are never seen again after the account is awarded.

Organization philosophy must be taken into account. Certain advertising agencies are known as highly creative shops; others base their programs on research and standard marketing practices. Some public relations organizations have a sound knowledge of business and the financial community, others are primarily concerned with celebrities. Some designers are apparently committed to ultramodern symbols, others can see value in existing packages and logotypes. Some research firms are mainly nose-counters, others have developed techniques for more penetrating studies. Managers should have a clear idea of what will be needed and look for counsel that can provide it.

In regard to accounts, the organization's compatability will be indicated by the programs it is handling. It is good practice to get a list of former accounts and check with them as well as with current clients. In addition, it is good policy to check with media and suppliers who know the work and reputation of most of the organizations in each field.

Then, too, the financial responsibility and the ability of any outside organization to pay its bills and maintain its organization should be established. Speaking of money, it is better to have a complete understanding about what is to be done and how much is to be paid before undertaking any outside service program. If work is to be done on a time basis, there should be reasonable estimates and limits set.

Sales presentations of many of the personal service organizations—advertising and public relations agencies, consultants, and designers—are notoriously colorful. A special language has been evolved by each group that is sometimes as flamboyant and mysterious as anything developed in government or educational circles.

Setting the Organization Structure

Other management decisions will be the organization structure for work on the corporate image, the place of public relations in the framework, the size and personnel of its department, the budget, and the direction of its activities. There is a growing realization that the corporate image is a long-range program and that public relations and advertising, as well as other communications, should be considered on a long-range rather than a short-term or emergency basis.

Another trend is toward the use of outside agencies or counsel for public relations. The corporate management retains responsibility, but uses the specialized skills and experience of trained people. If everyone in the company is busy, the best way to get effective and continuous programs is through an organization concentrating on communications.

Outsiders may also have more experience in handling changes or emergencies, such as government or other legal suits, requests to appear before government agencies, labor disputes, plant moves or closings, or physical disasters.

The appearances of company officers before government agencies or committees are increasingly important, and management should choose the persons who will represent the company and how statements will be prepared. Whether appearances are command performances or are set up by the company, there should be careful preparation and rehearsal for them.

In a number of companies, the functions and responsibilities of the communications staff are being increased. In a growing number of corporations, management is making regular checks of the attitudes of its people and the effectiveness of communications. At no time can this be more important than during a change in the image, and at no time is there a better opportunity to reach the entire organization.

Estimating the Costs

There are no general figures on the cost of an image program, because the requirements of each corporation will be different. It would be as difficult and unreasonable to estimate "average" costs as it would be to say that a certain amount is required for an advertising campaign or a plant investment. Each company, however, can make a reasonable estimate of its proposed program by analyzing the changes that are to be made and the elements of communications to be employed. Just as a matter of record, $50,000 seems to be a *minimum* for an examination of identity and preliminary work on graphics; $100,000 has been noted as the budget for a broader survey of the company image and preliminary recommendations. From these points there can be limitless expansion, with more than one campaign costing over $1 million, not including increased corporate advertising.

As has been shown, an image program may be simply a redirection of attitudes or communications if there are no major revisions of identity. At the other extreme, it can cover the entire range of identification and corporate personality, with completely new graphics, the support of corporate advertising and public relations, and increased costs of the internal organization and outside agencies.

If the program has been well analyzed and objectives established as they should be, the required elements are easy to visualize in advance. The costs can be determined and fitted into an overall budget.

It will be helpful to outline the successive steps that may be taken and the possible commitments for fees and costs. A new corporate image program will involve all or part of the people in certain departments, and their salaries and overhead can be estimated for a specified time. This should include executive supervision as well as management and department time.

The first step is usually examination of the corporation's existing image and identity and possibly preliminary recommendations for revisions. This will usually call for work by designers as well as the proposals of staff departments. Costs for various steps of design programs can be reasonably estimated. It should be considered whether these programs are to be extended to products and packages.

Research into public acceptance of the existing image and recognition of its identity may be done by an outside agency. The extent, duration, and expense of the work can be determined in advance.

To make possible an evaluation of existing and proposed images, a presentation for senior management or, perhaps, for the board of directors may be prepared. This calls for certain costs, depending on the amount of detail. Some presentations include extensive tests of identification on vehicles, buildings, and printed materials, and occasionally a film is used to dramatize the proposed changes.

If a complete change must be made quickly, there will be a substantial budget for stationery and other graphic materials, plant, office, and vehicle signs, education of employees and so on. Some corporations have been more deliberate, replacing plant signs as they come up for reconditioning and not adding special advertising to support the image.

Through standardization of colors and designs for signs, office and plant interiors, stationery and other materials, substantial economies have been made in some companies—enough in one case to offset much of the cost of the changes. The complete support and cooperation of the purchasing departments are always essential.

Advertising may be one of the principal expenses, depending on how extensive it is to be. The size of the campaign is usually determined by the nature and area of the business and the influence a new corporate image can have on sales and profits.

How to Check Results

Checking the results of an image program or any public relations campaign is difficult. Any assessment of results must relate to the objectives toward which the campaign was directed. It is unrealistic to aim the program or any segment of it toward one target and later survey another.

If the program is intended to create a new or more favorable image, an accurate measure of success depends on research before the program starts. This provides a bench mark against which later progress can be checked. It was recommended in Chapter 4 that such a preliminary survey be completely objective and that it be made by an outside organization. Subsequent surveys must be made with the same or an equal group of respondents to be meaningful.

For some corporations, a survey on the recognition of the firm or its trademarks may cover the results of a limited program. This is only a study of identification, not of reputation, but it can be significant.

One measure of specific programs is the price of the corporation stock before and after the campaign. Naturally, other factors will probably have as much or more effect on prices, but if the price-earnings ratio is appreciably higher, the program has been successful.

Publicity is one measure, but its value should be judged on what is published and in what media rather than on the number of inches of clippings. Other gauges are inquiries from publishers for news and articles and the unsolicited and favorable mentions of the firm. Corporations that have established a good reputation and handle emergency news capably can look good even in adversity.

Rapid turnover in employees, labor disputes, and problems in recruiting reflect an unfavorable image in most cases. Their improvement as a result of a sound program becomes another measure of success.

■　　■　　■

At this point, it is advisable to review those principles to be considered in planning and implementing an image program. There are 14 major points to remember.

1. The corporate image, as an integral and important part of management's functions, should be included in long-range planning.
2. A clear distinction should be made between the *image*, which exists in the minds of respondents, and an *identity*, which appears on

products, properties, vehicles, and in advertising and other communications.

3. Drastic changes taking place in the world—in society, the economy, government, finance, and management—make necessary periodic evaluation of the corporation's image.

4. There is a strong and growing relationship between a firm's image and its growth and prosperity.

5. Any successful campaign must have the strong support of senior management and be pushed throughout the entire organization.

6. An effective program should be based on careful research by capable, experienced people.

7. Objectives should be firmly set, audiences selected, and plans for execution of the program made before it is launched.

8. The best image programs are complete, not piecemeal. They should include every impression made by the company's products, personnel, properties, and communications.

9. All possible media should be used, particularly for new identity campaigns. All lines of communication, all contacts, and notifications should be charted in advance.

10. Special campaigns in the financial community should enlist the cooperation of shareholders, bankers, brokers, publishers, and potential investors.

11. All possible means should be used for employee education so that all workers become effective spokesmen for the corporation.

12. Every department of the firm should be drawn into the planning and promotion of the new image and continually used for further development.

13. The program should be regularly reviewed, by outside researchers where indicated, to show possible improvement and to assess results.

14. For most of the specialized aspects of the program, it is usually advisable to use outside talent. Within the organization, extreme care is needed in selecting personnel to handle an image program.

Three
Case Histories

Kaiser Aluminum & Chemical Corporation:
A New Image of Creativity

THIS case history reports the development and management of a program in which diverse parts have been combined into an unusually effective corporate image. Each element complements the others and adds strength to the whole. The program has been developed over a period of several years, and its influence is reflected in the opinions and actions of customers, employees, and investors.

There are two programs, parallel and mutually supporting, one for the corporate identity and one for the corporate image. Each has its own organization and objectives; both are closely linked in administration and in the planning of senior management.

Largest of the Kaiser enterprises and the subject of this case study is Kaiser Aluminum & Chemical Corporation. This company has grown and diversified extensively over its 25-year history. Although aluminum still represents almost 80 percent of its activity, other segments of the business are devoted to refractories, agricultural chemicals, nickel, special metals, secondary magnesium, iron ore, cattle, exploration, international trading, and property development.

In recent years, there have been alliances with other firms for development of resources, new ventures into building and land development, as

well as the addition of complete new product lines. The picture of Kaiser Aluminum is constantly changing.

The original Kaiser business started with road building and developed into major construction of such projects as Boulder Dam, shared with others of the Six Companies, an affiliation of six major contractors. In World War II, Kaiser built hundreds of merchant ships. For several years, there were Kaiser and Henry J. automobiles. Other Kaiser enterprises now include steel mills, mines, cement plants, construction and engineering organizations, chemicals, shipping, and jeeps and are located all over the world. These companies have separate managements and images, but there is a recognized relationship.

People at Kaiser Aluminum speak more about influence, communications, or performance than they do about a corporate image. This management subscribes to and strongly supports the concept that a modern corporation must keep pace with social as well as economic changes, that change is now the rule instead of the exception. At the same time, this is an organization of hard-nosed, tough-fibered men who are constantly fighting to improve the profitability of the company's products, seeking every possible means to improve production, develop resources, enter new fields, and reduce costs.

Kaiser is the most international of the U.S. firms in the aluminum industry and is probably the most diversified. It may be representative of many modern corporations, in which other managements will recognize many of the same opportunities and problems.

Management Leads Image Program

Here, the pace toward a new posture is set by management, and one management problem is priorities. What some planning people at Kaiser Aluminum want is a constant improvement in the company's performance, not only in sales and profits, but in its contributions to the peoples of the world. They feel that if an image can become static, it can get in the way of development, of innovation.

There is little probability that the image of Kaiser Aluminum will become anything but dynamic, whatever else it may be. This is a heritage of the founder, Henry J. Kaiser. Kaiser Aluminum and other enterprises carry his firm imprint.

Kaiser Center, the company headquarters in Oakland, California, is in many ways an image of the corporation. It is a reflection of the Kaiser family, of their feelings about Oakland, the West, and the local people. The firm has no manufacturing plants in the area, but Oakland was the hometown of the family and the headquarters of early Kaiser enterprises. Property was acquired that faces Lake Merritt, with enough land for an extensive garden and a large parking garage with another rooftop garden. The building is architecturally attractive and provides pleasant working conditions in an unusual setting.

On the first and second floors, which are open to the public, Kaiser Center has encouraged many exhibitions of art, painting, photography, and sculpture. Once a year, the works of Kaiser employees are hung, displaying a high degree of talent. The Center also provides facilities for community affairs and houses a bank, restaurants, and other conveniences for the neighborhood as well as for employees of all the Kaiser companies.

A pragmatic benefit of the Center is that it is an effective display of Kaiser products used in construction and shows Kaiser activities and products in a main-floor exhibit.

In just a quarter of a century, KACC has built a business grossing more than $850 million annually from the products of five continents. This is the same corporation that produced an Oscar-winning motion picture, *Why Man Creates*, which is universal in its appeal and presentation. It is a firm that devotes its external house organ to subjects such as world food shortages or today's youth. Improvement of the well-being of people in Jamaica and Ghana and the crisis in secondary education are among its many interests in public service.

At the same time, the picture seen by most outside observers is that of an aggressive newcomer in highly competitive industries, a worldwide entrepreneur, an organization that is growing and diversifying in several directions. This is the corporation for which an image program is evolving, one that may not yet be clear to everyone inside or outside the organization, but one that has definite objectives and strong executive support.

It is unlikely that any failure to recognize what Kaiser Aluminum is and what it stands for will long persist. Two fundamental policies underlie the programs that identify and characterize the corporation. First, the programs are to be complete. They are to involve everyone in the company, and they are to use every channel of communication. Second, the programs have the leadership and continued support of top management.

One of the major strengths of the Kaiser Aluminum program is the interlocking and mutual support of various elements. At the same time, it is completely clear, within the company and to others, that there are two distinctive programs—one for the corporate image and one for identity. Administrators of the two campaigns work closely together but have separate responsibilities and assignments.

The Identity Program

Because the identity program was under way first, and because it forms an important part of the foundation for a corporate image, this aspect of the company's efforts will be discussed first.

There was a general realization that identity needed to be improved and organized, and in 1961 T. J. Ready, Jr., then executive vice-president and now president of Kaiser Aluminum, asked the advertising and public affairs department to make a survey and report to senior management.

All forms of the company identification were assembled and placed on display in a then vacant floor of the Kaiser Center. Most of one floor was needed for the wide variety of signs, stationery, packages, advertising, annual reports, business forms, publications, business cards, and vehicle identifications.

The executive group that reviewed these displays agreed that there was a lack of uniformity among the designs of different categories; there was no discernible family resemblance between advertising, publications, and letterheads except for the use of the Kaiser name. Even the symbols had been used in various sizes and forms and changed in color, location, and association with the name and products. "The consensus of the viewers confirms that our company is not establishing a strong corporate identity with its current printed material" was the conclusion of a management memo in mid-1961.

A decision to work with an outside designer was based on convictions that professional assistance could help create an identity that would not become obsolete and would lend objectivity to the program.

In the previous decade, Kaiser Aluminum had used a number of design organizations, as had other affiliated companies. There had been one potential conflict between an identification for Kaiser automobiles and Mercedes-Benz, and other marks and symbols had been adopted, only to be dropped later. A new design organization was appointed for Phase 1 of the program, which would include research into existing materials, identification used by competitors and other firms, company policy, and expressions of the executive group.

The designers made their evaluation of identity names and symbols in use by Kaiser and other firms and offered a preliminary assortment of improvements. This was followed by discussions with company executives to establish the decisions that had to be made. It was quickly settled that all Kaiser companies, including Kaiser Aluminum, would continue to be identified by the family name so as to gain the greatest possible recognition from uniform identity and this well-known name.

Specific designs for divisions of Kaiser Aluminum were reviewed, and, at this point, the original assignment was concluded. The final designs were created by the company's art department, which worked with Henry J. Kaiser, Sr., Edgar F. Kaiser, and E. E. Trefethen, Jr., vice-chairman.

It is significant that since its inception the program has received strong, continuing support from the senior executive level. Approval of the stylized Kaiser trademark was given by the Kaisers, and the initiation of the campaign was announced thus by President D. A. Rhoades: "This program, including simplification and standardization of our printed material, will contribute materially to a strong and consistent visual identity for Kaiser Aluminum and all its divisions."

Simplification and standardization were key words in the announcement and have continued to be the basis of the expanding system. New firms, new products, and new markets have proliferated, calling for identification within a system that is no longer so simple but meets all contingencies.

The Identity Committee and the Identity System

Responsibility for the identity program was assigned to a corporate identity committee, headed by a member of the public affairs department and including one of the patent attorneys and a trademark attorney as well as graphics and communications personnel. Division advertising managers were soon appointed as members to work on their own problems and contribute their experience to the corporate program.

In addition to establishing a liaison with divisions and departments, the committee worked with the purchasing department for control of forms, packaging designs, and labels as well as other outside purchases, with materials handling for assistance in technical problems of packages, and with the international division for the redesign of all foreign identifications and registration of trademarks.

An immediate responsibility was the design of logotypes and selection of colors visually appropriate to the major trademark, an assignment that widened to include acceptable identifications for all the Kaiser companies.

The committee is immediately available to consider any problem presented by a division or department. The policy is to work out a satisfactory solution, acceptable to all, not to question whether a solution can be found.

The committee decided that an outside designer, who would work as a member of the group and be familiar with all the problems and possibilities, would be a valuable addition. A number of organizations were considered before Mary B. Sheridan and Associates of Los Angeles was selected, a choice that has demonstrated its effectiveness over more than six years.

Both the image and identity programs have been evolutions rather than revolutions. There has been no need for a crash program or drastic changes, because there has been no change in the company name or the major categories of business. As the company continues to diversify and expand, both in this country and around the world, there has been a broadening of the picture it presents and accommodations in the way it is identified.

Because the program has been flexible and gradual, it has been possible to coordinate all parts of a widely diversified business through all the channels of communication with employees, stockholders, the financial community, customers, and the general public. This has been done with minimum disruption and maximum impact because it has always been an important part of long-range planning.

The identity program is now established as a corporation-wide system that anticipates all possibilities and makes solutions possible before problems develop. There have been only a few situations that simply did not fit into the system.

The basis of the system is the corporate logotype, in which the Kaiser name is always dominant and is being increasingly emphasized. This logotype is used throughout the business by companies, divisions, joint ventures, and subsidiaries.

As the trademark and principal identification of all companies, the name Kaiser is designed in a subtle but characteristic hand-lettered form, for which there is no exactly matching typeface. No deviation or abbreviation is permitted. There are primary marks for each company, developed with the cooperation of legal and patent departments, but no letter or design symbol as such. The letter "K" may not be used to stand for Kaiser.

Color has been made a point of distinction. For identification of the principal divisions in Kaiser Aluminum, there is a color code that embraces all subdivisions. As an example, a standard red is used for aluminum and for products of such subdivisions as Kaiser Aluminum Roofing & Siding and Kaiser Aluminum Culvert. Other colors are green for chemicals, gold for refractories, purple for nickel, brown for bauxite, and blue for magnesium. This extends to advertising and literature, packages, plant signs, sales promotion, and business forms and reports.

For plant areas, logotypes are adapted to stationery, business cards and office forms, checks, and price pages. In all these forms, there is a

The identity system is extended to all the divisions and subdivisions of Kaiser, with a distinctive logotype for each and a separate color for each division.

KAISER ALUMINAS

KAISER ALUMINUM ROOFING & SIDING

KAISER ALUMINUM BUILDING PRODUCTS

KAISER ALUMINUM HOUSE SIDING

KAISER ALUMINUM ELECTRICAL PRODUCTS

KAISER ALUMINUM ROD, BAR & WIRE

KAISER ALUMINUM EXTRUSIONS

KAISER ALUMINUM SHEET & PLATE

KAISER ALUMINUM FOIL

KAISER ALUMINUM RAIN CARRYING SYSTEM

KAISER ALUMINUM FOIL & CONTAINERS

KAISER ALUMINUM CULVERT

KAISER ALUMINUM INGOT

KAISER ALUMINUM RIGID FOIL CONTAINERS

KAISER ALUMINUM HIGHWAY PRODUCTS

KAISER INSTITUTIONAL FILM

KAISER FOIL

KAISER INSTITUTIONAL FOIL

KAISER ALUMINUM CONSUMER PRODUCTS

KAISER FILM #8

fixed design in which the logotype must appear in specified size and position and in the true division color, if color is used. On stationery, all addresses and other designations except the corporate name and executive title are placed at the bottom of the page for a more flexible design.

Standard formats have not been generally extended to advertising—though the logotype must be used in standard form—but the advertising department and the agency are working on plans to achieve a more general uniformity of Kaiser advertising.

Only photographic reproduction of the trademark is permitted, to insure exact duplication. The hand-lettered "Kaiser" is used only in the logotype, not in headlines or body copy. Approved typefaces and their related sizes are specified. Other instructions in the identity manual discuss the use of logotypes in advertising, in printed materials, and on sales promotion pieces.

With so many ramifications in the new product lines, the words "aluminum" and "chemical" do not always describe the activity. As a result, there will be occasions when the formal corporate designation must be modified where it is not applicable, and where the name "Kaiser" must be emphasized.

Application of the identity system to packaging was one of the later and more difficult developments, as well as one that the company considers of major importance. The tremendous number of products, in a variety of shapes and sizes, and almost every type of commercial container, presented a challenge as well as an opportunity. How to gain attention and recognition for so many goods, from plant to consumer, was the problem of the identity committee.

In spite of the variations in size and shape, successful packaging systems for each division have been worked out using the Kaiser trademark and standard division colors. In addition to the standard colors, others have been selected for use on special packages and provided through central purchasing.

In the aluminum division, general recognition has been gained for products ranging from nails to cable to roofing through use of the color red and a distinctive wedge pattern. Similar systems are in effect for refractories, chemicals, and other industrial products.

In addition to its principal trademark, the company uses a number of secondary marks for which specific instructions are also in effect. It is pointed out that the protection of each mark depends on proper usage. Rules for the combination of secondary marks with Kaiser have been formulated. It is also required that in development or prospective registration of any new trademarks, the patent department be advised in advance of any expense for design or promotion.

Persuasion and Assistance Employed

Compliance with identity standards is expected throughout the company and there are few exceptions, but this compliance is gained through persuasion and assistance rather than rigid policing methods. When there is a problem of design or the need for a color change in printed materials, packages, or elsewhere, the identity committee works hard to find acceptable suggestions within the specifications.

The corporation frequently paid the initial cost of designs and planning and made materials available to all divisions and subdivisions. The costs of materials and labor for signs and other identification at division or plant level are charged to the profit center concerned. When the time for major changes is not opportune, there is no emphasis on speed, but there is no compromise on the quality of identification or the exact reproduction of set designs.

One of the harder problems has come with acquisition of other companies that have their own long-established trademarks, colors, and package designs or with the formation of joint ventures and subsidiaries that include other established identities.

Entry into agricultural chemicals was through acquisition of an established company whose management felt that its brands and identification should be continued. Over a period of time, a mutually satisfying program was worked out that retained as much as possible of the existing identity but brought the new division under the Kaiser name and colors.

An important new venture is Kaiser-Aetna, which specializes in land development. The Aetna Life Insurance Company name was well-known and valuable and could not be lost in the amalgamation. The result is a logotype for Kaiser-Aetna, which retains the distinctive lettering of both firms.

In other cases, gradual and relatively minor adjustments are made, and more emphasis may be given to the name Kaiser. This makes possible the identification of new firms and products in the Kaiser family without long and involved signatures.

In such solutions of identity problems, whether for new companies or revised packages, there has been no compromise with design quality. All the necessary time and many preliminary designs have been made available. As a policy, the company is committed to doing each step the right way, even if this care causes the program to move at a slower pace.

The guidebook for the identity program, *Corporation Identity Policies*, opens with an explanation of the significance of a strong, favorable identity, states the principles on which Kaiser Aluminum's program is based, recognizes the relationship with other Kaiser enterprises, and affirms the strong sponsorship of management. The committee is identified and channels of contact explained. The manual goes on to describe and illustrate the system of logotypes and colors. Injunctions against deviations are spelled out, and instructions are given for typefaces and other format regulations. In conclusion, the guidebook says,

> The successful application of the corporate identity plan will not only improve our company's public "image" but the standardization of design and printing will save money. This brochure cannot cover all the possible applications of the principles of this plan. The corporate identity committee welcomes the opportunity to assist in any way in interpreting or reviewing these policies with respect to any particular design or identification problem.

Anniversary Prompts Image Program

In its relatively brief (25 years) corporate life, Kaiser Aluminum has had varying images and diverse identifications—all, however, under the Kaiser name. Problems of standardization have been multiplied by the acquisition of other companies with well-known names and Kaiser's entry into new fields, so thousands of products and packages had to be integrated into the corporate identity.

Sporadic attempts to define the corporate image and find an acceptable way to express what the company represents were made during most of its earlier life. After the identity policies were initiated in 1961–1962, there were more active discussions, leading to the creation of various slogans and symbols, none of which was generally popular.

The occasion that brought all these projections into focus and started the present successful program was the twentieth anniversary of the firm in 1966. When appropriate means of marking this event were considered, there was a general feeling that rather than merely recording the brief two decades, taking a look at the future was in order. This feeling sparked enough ideas in the public affairs and communications organizations, as well as among the senior executives, so that specific suggestions took form and were joined for a true image program. It was then possible to record policies and plans. Excerpts from a report of the vice-president, public relations, follow.

> Kaiser Aluminum & Chemical Corporation is dedicated to continued growth and increasing profitability in its business of transforming ores and basic chemicals into key products to fill the needs of industry and agricultural markets of the United States and the free world. . . .

Further diversification is a basic corporate policy, with emphasis on areas that are extensions of, or related to, the corporation's present business and demonstrated strengths. . . .

At the same time, it is also our objective to be responsive to worldwide social responsibilities, to have special regard for the public interest, to preserve the constructive challenges and responsibilities of the American enterprise system, and to mitigate the growth of government restraints. Through the development of suitable information and community relations programs, the company will make a special effort to insure that the public understands and approves of its policies and actions. . . .

Future corporate activity will be based on experience and capabilities gained in the past; at the same time, it is recognized that our past accomplishments are modest when compared to what we are confident can be done in the foreseeable future.

How the objectives were to be implemented in a corporate image program was stated as follows in a brief report.

A coordinated communications program of public relations, advertising, and internal communications was established. Its basic elements included:

1. A unique theme that expressed the company's "future" outlook in a simple, forceful manner.
2. A detailed schedule of year-round communications activities that employed the basic theme in all media.

The importance of ideas and the need to forecast the future were brought together in the main theme, sometimes expressed by such slogans as "The Idea Is Ideas" and "Creativity." A silhouette of a head was designed as a graphic theme and used in visual materials. Corporate advertising, the external house organ, motion pictures, public and community affairs, financial contacts, and publicity were all allied to carry the corporate image in the same direction.

The year-long observance was inaugurated in December 1965 by President T. J. Ready, Jr. An original forecasting game called Future was created and distributed to many customers, government leaders, students, educators, and investors. Plant observances were held in all plants that were 20 years old. All activities and promotion ideas were publicized in local and national media.

Film Reflects Pace of Change

The company has recognized the pace of change, not only in itself but in the national and world economies, social conditions and human prob-lems, methods of doing business, new elements of competition, expan-sion around the globe. This attitude is expressed in the introduction to the Kaiser film, *Why Man Creates.*

> The environment in which we function is a competitive one. We com-pete for sales, for qualified employees, for funds to expand our busi-ness, for a number of things that others need too. So, to be competi-tive in obtaining these resources, we must find ways of conducting our business more effectively than our competitors.

> Industry's application of the new technologies has brought the mechanical problems of business pretty well under control. But in ap-plying that technology, industry has helped increase the rate of change. And now, change is taking place at such an accelerated rate that people and companies are hard pressed to keep up with it. Ideas good enough to last for a thousand years a century ago, today appear, are used, then discarded in months.

> To be competitive, a company must be committed to face and chal-lenge these tremendous changes. It needs to be willing to turn in the comfortable, tested solutions and apply new ones. It needs to encour-age its employees to question and experiment, regardless of what task they do. The company and its employees must be able to cope with change. And coping with change isn't a bad definition of creativity.

Why Man Creates is one of the outstanding elements in the broad program that presents Kaiser Aluminum concepts and policies. This film often prompts the question, "Why does a company like yours sponsor a film like this?" The film is a colorful journey through the unpredictable world of creativity; sometimes puzzling, often exciting, always fascinat-ing. Among the 24 awards it has received is an Oscar for the best docu-mentary short subject of 1968. Even more significant is the record of show-ings and the response of audiences around the world.

The reasons for making this picture are set forth in a statement that first outlines the company's diversification in a score of countries. The statement continues, "So we have changed—and rather substantially. What has this to do with the film?" The answer is a discussion of change, of competition, and of the necessity of coping with change. It reaches this conclusion:

The "creativity" film and the projects that led up to it show how this concern for changes has been presented within our company. Kaiser Aluminum was 20 years old in 1966. And to mark this event, our management felt it would be more productive to spend the advertising and public relations budgets looking ahead to the next 20 years, rather than fondly reminiscing about those gone by.

Kaiser Aluminum uses pictures for many purposes. In its inventory of motion pictures and slide films, there are distributor training films, films on aspects of management for supervisors, profiles of specific markets, films about communications, sales aid and salesmanship presentations, and various technical pictures. There are also general-interest movies, of which the creativity film is the star. Motion pictures have been a consistent and effective means of communication and image building for the company.

Publication Programs

There are two publication programs, one for the education and assistance of employees and representatives and another to attract and influence opinion leaders, people in government, and investors.

Several divisions of the company have their own publications for present and potential customers and are part of a hard-hitting sales promotion program. These are edited in the divisions and sent to mailing lists prepared from sales and prospect reports. In principal plant areas, company newspapers are prepared by the local organizations. Headquarters has commented that these publications could be more useful in educating employees and that plans will move in that direction.

From Kaiser Center, a corporate newsletter, *News Notes,* goes to nearly 8,000 headquarters employees, field sales offices, and plant management employees. A weekly distribution of press clippings goes to a similar list. Annual publications include a detailed report on all Kaiser organizations and a condensed information brochure for employees.

A truly unique company publication that has attracted international attention is the *Kaiser News,* published since World War II as a corporate house organ. There is no mention of aluminum or any other Kaiser product. Current issues discuss in depth some phases of American life and institutions. The magazine is strikingly illustrated in full color, and the subject treatment would do credit to any review.

Circulation of the *News* may reach 100,000 or more and includes executives of leading corporations, financial institutions, many federal administrative agencies, all members of Congress, U.S. information outlets overseas, embassy libraries, administrative and legislative officials in the 37 states in which Kaiser Aluminum has operations, mass media, and universities. The *News* is available on request, and interested groups may place bulk orders at a nominal rate. One issue reached a circulation of 500,000.

As part of the twentieth anniversary program, six issues discussed "The Dynamics of Change" and were later published in book form. Emphasizing the creativity theme of the company's program, one issue was titled "The Corporation as a Creative Environment," and another, "You and Creativity," again explored the nature of creativity.

One of the most popular issues was "The Children of Change," a detailed report on young people seeking to bring about radical changes in the Establishment. It was introduced this way:

> [It] examines in detail this nonverbal, nonintellectual movement . . . the movement's art, music, literature, fashion, and the underground press are all studied. A new life style that many of them have adopted —the commune—is also discussed from the vantage point of personal visits to several communes.

The editor of the News reports only to the public relations vice-president and to the corporation president and has wide latitude in selection and preparation of the material. Some of the issues represent the work of a year or more.

Advertising Supports the Image Program

Kaiser Aluminum's corporate advertising is a current example of the coordination of various communications channels, the linking of company publications and media advertising to strengthen the interest and appeal of both. Institutional advertising is separated from the product advertising of each division, and division advertising is related to the corporate message whenever that is practical.

The program for 1970 is distinctive in appearance as well as in content. Before the campaign was created, these goals were stated to the department and the agency:

1. Increase the awareness, understanding, and favorable opinions of the broad capabilities of Kaiser Aluminum & Chemical Corporation and its divisions in businessmen and other selected groups.

2. Support the public interest objectives of the corporation.
3. Identify and promote selected major products and markets illustrative of our principal business activities.
4. Provide opportunities for divisions to tie in to the corporate program with their own merchandising activities.
5. Achieve more unity and impact of total communications efforts by interrelating subjects and graphic treatments of *Kaiser Aluminum News,* corporate and divisional advertising.
6. Create dominant, impressive, distinctly different advertisements in a series which is characteristically identifiable with our company and the image it wants to project.

Target audiences were selected and defined and the message that the campaign should convey to these audiences was spelled out. The messages included the broad capabilities of the corporation, diversified interests in products and markets, major activities in aluminum, potential new areas of growth, and involvement in social responsibilities.

Six major advertisements were used in 1970, each a series of four consecutive pages in full color, in news, business, and industrial magazines. Plans were worked out for each advertisement and the corresponding issue of the Kaiser *News* to have the same subject and related graphic treatment. In the magazine, the subject is considered in depth to evoke broad human interest and public concern. The advertisement opens with the general theme and presents corporate involvement in the needs and problems. Topics are the general world environment, then specific subjects such as shelter, energy, food, transportation, and communications.

Together, the *News* and the advertisements illustrate how the subject concerns company customers, business executives, investors, government, educators, and the press. "Markets of Change" was the subject of the first advertisement and the first issue of the *News* in the series. It discussed the ideas of development, progress, how the concept that man "owns" the earth is undergoing reexamination.

The advertisement on shelter illustrates and describes "a street where the world lives," from grass huts to glass houses, adobe to aluminum, hovels to high-rise apartment houses. On the subject of food, two problems are discussed: Grow enough to go around, and then, get it around. Store it, ship it, and serve it.

Of the campaign, the corporation's advertising agency, Young & Rubicam, makes this comment:

KACC wants its reputation to extend well beyond the literal meaning of the name "aluminum and chemical corporation" to include what it wants to be, and is becoming: a highly diversified corporation with a broad sense of responsibility. . . . It wants to be known for imagination, daring, ingenuity, underscored by a strong tradition of pragmatism.

Henry Kaiser said, "find a need and fill it." In 1970 the corporation has defined the world's needs in terms of major markets. It presents these markets in terms of social needs and defines them in a broad sense and then relates specific Kaiser projects to those needs. . . . In this total sense, Kaiser moves toward two objectives: a broad corporate identity and specific, divisional product selling.

The Community and Government Relations

Another active and strongly organized group in the public affairs and communications field is charged with community relations and government contacts. It is primarily a field organization under policy direction from corporate headquarters. Three regional offices for Kaiser Aluminum are in Louisiana, the Midwest, and the Pacific Northwest. Joint offices with other Kaiser companies are in Washington, D.C. and California.

Kaiser has always worked closely with government; many of its early activities, such as the building of Liberty ships, were commissioned by the government. Management knows the importance of maintaining good lines of communication with government bureaus and departments, and this is one of the important phases of its public affairs offices.

The company points out that the work of this department is not primarily defensive. On the whole it is oriented toward advance planning. For example, in anticipation of stronger control of air pollution, Kaiser Aluminum is working with other companies both to develop improved technology and to gain reasonable regulations and fair administration.

Headquarters support for the active staff is supplied through task forces, bringing together members of various divisions or departments that will be affected by the problem. In the field, particularly in regard to community relations, much responsibility is given local executives on the basis that the people who live with the situation are best equipped to plan and act.

The degree of this participation by local people does depend on their ability and inclination as well as the size of the operation. In Jamaica, one of the principal sources of bauxite for the company, local managers have for years been active and effective members of the community. When a new enterprise is set up, such as land development, advance knowledge of the community is obtained and trained people are assigned.

Contribution policies are set at headquarters. Plants and divisions make recommendations for their budgets; once this is established, any amount over $50 must have home-office approval. The company considers the United Fund–Community Chest organizations to be most effective in their plant areas. It is explained that unregulated donations would set examples for other solicitations and disrupt both local and total budgets and programs.

The Financial Community Is Informed

In addition to covering the financial community through advertising and publications, the public relations department is charged with direct and mail contacts with stockholders, brokers, analysts, bankers, and others in the investment world.

There have been a good many announcements of expansion and other activities, and more are anticipated. A strong effort is being made to synchronize delivery of these announcements to all channels. Distribution by telegram, messenger, or air mail is carefully controlled to make sure that analysts and news services have the word as soon as it appears on the broad tape.

Under a new policy, quarterly earnings figures are sent in special mailings to stockholders and others, as soon as possible after they are available, and ahead of dividend payments. There have been promotion materials used with dividend mailings, and others are planned.

Senior officers of the company hold both formal and informal meetings with analysts, bankers, and others whenever possible. The annual report has always been considered more than a record of financial affairs. It reports in considerable detail on many of the company's activities, reviewing what has taken place and outlining plans for the future. In format, the report is conservative, and is highly readable.

Corporate publicity is also the function of the public relations department, with special emphasis on corporate and financial developments. News of personnel, introduction of products, and other items of interest to customers and prospects are developed by the advertising and PR personnel of plants and divisions.

Clearance of news releases is strictly controlled. News of only local interest can be approved and issued at that level, but any announcement of national interest or about company policy must be cleared by the division and then headquarters. If there is any question of legal, patent, financial, or industrial relations, clearance must first come from the appropriate department, and major announcements are then passed to the president's office for approval.

Technical and business articles about the company, or articles by members of the organization, are encouraged. Again, first clearance is at division level, and a decision is made there as to the need for higher approval. Most technical material and general articles are checked by the public affairs department to avoid possible duplication and prevent misstatements of company policy or untimely disclosure of information.

One survey of the financial community's attitude toward Kaiser Aluminum has been made and shows what the company considers a satisfactory response. General approval of the public image program is best demonstrated by its continuing enthusiastic support. Response from target audiences has been consistently growing, specifically in the number of groups viewing company motion pictures and the number of requests for house organs. The book containing the first six issues of the *News* received wide distribution. Feature articles on the "Future" theme were carried by daily newspapers with total circulation of nearly three million. More than 3,000 letters were received after distribution of the Future game.

Kaiser Aluminum feels that the direction of its image program is well established and the presentation of the company will be one of steady development. It is evident that KACC has much to tell its target audiences and will have a great deal more in the future. It has created an effective organization and unusual means of communication through which this continuing story will be told. There is a high degree of coordination between advertising, publications, publicity, films, and public affairs, so that all move toward the desired result. Probably the most important fact is that the corporate image, by whatever name the company wishes to call it, has become an integral part of long-range programming and has the continued and strong support of management and the board of directors.

Crown Zellerbach Corporation:
A New Mark for a New Century

CROWN Zellerbach Corporation was 100 years old in 1970. As part of the Centennial commemoration, the company introduced a new identity system, featuring a new corporation symbol and signature. The occasion was also marked by release of an outstanding company motion picture, special publications, and new approaches to public relations.

It was not without reservations, at least in some quarters, that Crown Zellerbach assumed a new identity. In its hundred-year history, the company has gained general approval and respect from customers, employees, and investors. The headquarters building in San Francisco has been widely acclaimed as an outstanding use of city space and good architectural design. The policy of welcoming the public to Crown Zellerbach forests has won friends throughout the West.

The company has expanded in this country and abroad and is a major factor in its industries. Members of the CZ organization have been active in public and civic affairs. There have been no recent changes that demand new identification. In presenting a new mark, a new signature, and other modifications of the corporate image, the company was bidding from strength.

In contrast to some industrial companies, Crown Zellerbach has a broad line of consumer and institutional products, is known by brand to millions of customers, and is in close contact with distributors as well as industrial buyers. For all these people there has been a favorable image of the firm for many years.

Uniformity Needed

What were the reasons, then, for a long-established firm to don new dress? One of the strongest was the lack of uniform identification. The trademark was gradually evolved from earlier symbols, and various divisions and consolidations have done business under eight different corporate symbols. The new program was set up to improve and standardize the corporate identity and to bring into sharper focus the picture of a 100-year-old organization that has kept pace with the demands and opportunities of economic and social changes.

In its recommendations for a distinctive and uniform identity system, the communications department showed how many variations were in use, concluding its argument this way:

> You will see that in the absence of a corporate identification system there is a fair degree of inconsistency and a rather high degree of interpretation. . . . Even less attention has been paid to uniform styling of the name. And yet in the last analysis the name of the company is really more important than the symbol.

> We do not have a corporate signature as such. That is, there is no agreement on the way in which the symbol is used in combination with the company name. This makes us look like a minor leaguer, rather than the billion-dollar corporation we are. We do not accurately project our modern facilities, new technology, new lines of business and new management.

Predecessors of Crown Zellerbach were established as early as 1870 in the Columbia and Willamette river valleys of Oregon, the central valley of California, and San Francisco. A. Zellerbach & Sons later became Zellerbach Paper Company, a division that is still active, and then merged with Crown Willamette Company to form Crown Zellerbach. The new company grew further by internal development and other acquisitions.

As the organization broadened its activities, trademark designs reflected the changes for the same reason that the company now introduces a modern identification. With due respect for history and tradition, CZ management knows that change is necessary, as much for its posture as for technical and market developments.

Since 1953 the familiar "Crown over CZ" has been used; it is based on a traditional adaptation. The first mark was a diamond with a Z, for A. Zellerbach & Co. The crown came from Crown Willamette, following a 1928 merger. The most recently used symbol was first designed by a sales division and became the corporate mark by adoption.

Problems of Differentiation

In addition to its need for standardization and more accurate representation, CZ was motivated by the examples of other corporations in the forest-products industry. Within the last few years, a number of these firms have introduced modern identities through effective programs.

It is interesting that Weyerhaeuser, Boise Cascade, and International Paper retain some identification with the forest and use stylized trees in their corporate symbols, while MacMillan Bloedel moved to an initial, as did Scott Paper. All new symbols are far removed from former identifications, and all reflect the industry's expansion into widely varied products and services. In all its earlier symbols, CZ had never used a tree.

The company may not have pictured a tree, but there are few variations of a crown that did not appear, either in marks of former companies or uncontrolled designs for plants or divisions. The regal Z at the start of the century was modified in a series of Crown Zs that culminated in the 1953 design, which was adapted to consumer products as well as the corporate identification.

In the meantime, Crown Zellerbach Canada had issued guidelines for identification of plants and other materials that resulted in better standardization than the parent company's, and Zellerbach Paper Company in 1967 created an independent system, used on printed materials, vehicles, and other items.

One finding of the communications department was that since the use of a crown for company or product identification was extremely widespread, it would be very hard to create or adapt a crown design that would not be conflicting or confusing. Hundreds of crowns and coronets were easily found, principally on consumer packages, to illustrate this problem. Products range from liquor, beer, and wine to cigarettes and cigars, toiletries, foods, watches and other accessories, luggage, batteries, automobiles, gasoline, and floor coverings. Airlines, banks, electric shavers, soaps, and margarines all are identified with crown designs.

It was apparent that any mark based on or including a crown was certain to run into conflicts or confusion in some branch of industry or some part of the world. Therefore, it was recommended that the proposed new symbol be abstract rather than representational and that it depart completely from former emblems and signatures. As a result, one of the major decisions was to bury the crown with honors.

Another was to standardize the company name as Crown Zellerbach without the word "Corporation" in the identification system. As noted by the communications department, variations of the company name in printed material and on properties were even more confusing than the symbols. CZ Corporation, Crown Z, Crown-Zellerbach, and others appeared on plants and equipment. In corporate advertising, the signature was Crown Zellerbach, in industrial ads it was Crown Zellerbach Corporation. Consumer products advertising eliminated both the company signature and symbol. In the first proposal to management, it was pointed out that "It is not the company emblem, but the company name that projects the corporation reputation to customers, stockholders, employees, potential recruits, the financial and business community, and local operating areas."

Current Representation Needed

So it became recognized throughout the organization that existing identification and perhaps other phases of the corporate image failed to properly represent this large, progressive, and socially conscious company. Consideration of the hundredth anniversary offered an effective opportunity to bring the corporate mark into a new century and, at the same time, make possible a centennial celebration that highlighted the modern image. At this point an executive decision was made to complete Phase 1 of the proposed program consisting of a thorough examination of the existing company identification, of current developments in competing and other industries, and of the means by which a new system would be evolved. Considerations of time and budgets were made.

To support recommendations for the new identity system, the communications department spent several months on the preliminary presentation, or Phase 1. As offered to management this included two volumes— one reviewing the research to that point and the other, graphic exhibits.

Covered in the first were reports on industry trends and statements on identity programs from authoritative sources, the evolution of the CZ trademark and variations in the symbols and logotypes, the broad purpose of a new system and its implementation, estimates of time and costs, considerations of legal and patent criteria, and options available to the company in considering a new identification.

Recommendations were supported by interviews with other companies, revised identity programs of firms in the paper and packaging business as well as others in different industries, statements by chief executives on their new campaigns, research considerations that included professional surveys, and excerpts from articles about corporate identity.

The second volume reproduced material from several identity manuals and showed their use in guiding a program, the various marks and symbols which the existing Crown Zellerbach identity had developed, variations and misuse of the company signature, examples of the different systems by which a revised identity could be created, illustrations of many of the crowns used commercially, and samples of identification in the firm's advertising.

Members of the design organization visited a number of the company's principal plants in different parts of the country and Canada, and pictures were obtained of other operations.

To complete Phase 1, alternative possibilities were outlined for management consideration. These were primarily the options available to any corporation that is not forced into change by merger or other major development. They included standardization of existing marks and signatures, modification of the symbol and logotype, creation of a completely new identity, use of the company name without a symbol, and a change in the corporate name.

The objectives of the company were stated by Robert G. Rogers, president of Crown Zellerbach Canada, who reviewed the development program before an international management meeting of the company early in 1970. He said, in part:

> We began searching for a suitable trademark and corporate identity program about two years ago to serve as a unifying umbrella—a set of identification standards—for all of our operations around the world. Soon, whenever you see our new symbol, it will clearly identify a company, plant, or branch office as part of a unified global organization.

> The system establishes uniformity in the styling and display of the company name and trademark on buildings and other properties, transportation equipment, advertising and other promotional materials, stationery, forms, packaging, institutional literature and their uses on radio and television.

> What factors were considered in the final choice of a symbol? Clarity and simplicity. We—and here I refer to a cross-section of senior management people in various parts of the CZ organization—considered a number of designs and the final one was based on subjective judgments and personal tastes. We wanted a symbol that would capture the company's forward movement, its spirit of innovation

and aggressiveness, its growth and diversification, and its readiness to change.

At the conclusion of Phase 1, the following recommendations were made to senior management and approved.

- To retain the name Crown Zellerbach as it does not date or limit the company and is a unique and widely recognized corporate name.
- To create a new trademark that has no relation to former symbols but will more accurately represent the corporation as a progressive, successful organization. The emblem should be suitable wherever the company is identified.
- To select and standardize company colors for the symbol and for other appropriate uses.
- To assign the design of a trademark and corporate logotype to a recognized organization, preferably one in California.

Other major policies were also approved: that the identity system be complete throughout the corporation and its subsidiaries, that it be implemented as rapidly as economically practical, and that the program have the strong and continued support of senior management.

New Mark Based on Research

Phase 2 of the program was started with the appointment of an outside design organization, authorizing it to study the company's identification needs, its possibilities, and limitations. One early step of the design organization was the preparation of a complete chart of the company's properties and structure to show every point at which identification would be established or where there would be any communication with other departments or the outside. This involved months of travel, photography, scale-model building, analysis of existing nomenclature and the possibility of standardization.

As in any new identity system, there were considerations of its use in foreign countries, legal and patent studies, packaging applications for consumer and industrial products, and the involvement of virtually all parts of the corporate organization from resources and production to marketing and advertising. This was the continuing work of the communications department and company executives with the designers to present a comprehensive, quickly effective, system.

These months of preparatory work culminated in the formal pres-

To show applications of the new identity symbol, Crown Zellerbach had scale models built and actual equipment painted in advance.

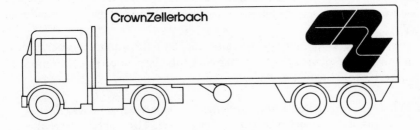

This special symbol, marking the hundredth year of Crown Zellerbach, was widely used during the 1970 celebration.

entation of the new identity symbol and its applications to senior management. To show the system in use as dramatically as possible, a brief motion picture was made. This called for advance painting of signs, vehicles, railroad cars, tanks, and all types of properties and equipment, as well as applications on stationery, forms, publications, and other media.

The theme of the picture was "to see ourselves as others see us" wherever Crown Zellerbach operates in this country and abroad. Some of the effects were accomplished with models, but for full impact the camera follows actual equipment into the woods and in factories, on logging roads and freeways, and into a wide variety of activities at corporate headquarters.

Following selection and management approval of the new symbol and signature, the program moved into Phase 3, the establishment and implementation of the system. This was introduced during the course of a three-day management conference in January 1970.

In addition to presentations and discussion of these proposals, the group attended the first showing of the corporate motion picture, saw advance illustrations of special publications for the Centennial Year, and viewed an extensive slide presentation of various applications of the new identity. This introduction was given by R. G. Rogers, president of Crown Zellerbach Canada, who discussed the desired impact on the various publics in which Crown Zellerbach is involved: customers and distributors, employees and potential personnel, investors and the financial community, various branches of government, and the total consuming public.

Mr. Rogers pointed out the importance of the younger generation in the long-range plans of the company and the impact of this group on the future. He told the management group:

> It is important that Crown Zellerbach not only act in a way that is consistent with society's wishes, but that we also appear to act this way. The public forms a picture of a company from a lot of little impressions, not only of its performance, but also from its appearance.

> It is obvious that the ability of virtually any company to expand its share of the market, to raise the new capital it needs to grow and prosper, is inevitably affected by the public's attitude toward it. . . .

> The objective of our corporate identity program is to help the company project a more accurate, unified, and favorable impression. All the bits and pieces, all the communications that emanate from Crown Zellerbach must be gathered together and made into a consistent whole.

> Then the corporate personality, our image, will register more effectively. It will have significance in the minds of people. It will be a unique image that stands out from the multitude of others and truly reflects Crown Zellerbach.

Broader Aspects of Image

In a discussion of the broader aspects of the corporate image, President Rogers pointed out that the attitude of the public, and particularly of specific groups and organizations, is widely recognized as a major factor in management planning. He made the following points.

> Part of this attention to public image is what might be called a preventive measure; that is, an industry with a good reputation—and we as part of that industry—is less likely to be the target of restrictive legislation or organized protests that will inhibit operations.

> But there is also a more positive aspect, one which relates to the highly competitive state of the marketplace today. Great quantities of products of similar function, quality, and price are pouring into warehouses

and stores. Moreover, they are marketed by competing manufacturers with much the same merchandising and advertising practices.

In our present environment, consumers, shareholders, employees, the press, the business and financial community are no longer merely interested in past performance or in product quality and price alone. They are asking more and more: What is the reputation of the company? The nature of the organization? What are the characteristics of the company as reflected by its management? How does it relate to its environment? Where is it headed?

The need is for a strong, positive public image which will help to provide a climate in which an organization's activities can be more successfully carried out.

It is clearly recognized by Crown Zellerbach management that the corporate image is not something to be created and superimposed on the organization, but rather it is an accurate reflection of what the company actually is, a reflection of management's thoughts and actions.

The new identity system and commemoration of the Centennial are recognized as visual means for expressing the corporate image and an opportunity for which the organization has been carefully prepared.

At the end of its first 100 years, Crown Zellerbach is a broadly diversified and integrated firm, second largest in the pulp and paper industry, with 33,000 stockholders, nearly 28,000 employees, and 1969 sales of $919,282,000. Expansion has been both domestic and international and includes packaging, consumer sanitary and disposable products, modern business and data processing papers, and a wide line of paper for industrial, institutional, and agricultural uses.

Newsprint is a major product of Canadian and Northwest mills. New techniques for coating magazine papers resulted in a joint venture with Time Inc. in Louisiana, with an investment exceeding $64 million. The Gaylord division, growing out of a 1955 merger, has shipping-container plants in key markets throughout the country. More recent developments include plastic and foil packaging and wraps for the food industries and multiwall bags, in addition to a fast-growing line of tissues, towels, and napkins. For these consumer products, CZ is the market leader in the 13 western states. Building materials and chemicals from wood are growing divisions of the business. In 1969, a new plant in Washington started production of disposable, nonwoven fabric, primarily for institutional uses.

Few large corporations have demonstrated keener concern about the challenges of a rapidly changing world. In principle and practice, Crown Zellerbach has been known as a good employer, a fair competitor, and a firm with which both customers and suppliers like to do business. This alone is not enough. In the 1968 annual report, the firm published a special supplement, "The Public Responsibility of Private Enterprise." Its introduction read as follows.

> Private business has long recognized that it has both rights and responsibilities as a corporate citizen. In recent years, the question of properly defining the public responsibilities of private enterprise has taken on new importance as a result of the broad social and economic problems confronting our industrial society.

> The business community is actively seeking new ways to contribute to the solution of these problems within the framework of the competitive economic system. . . . Crown Zellerbach considers such activities—supported by the necessary expenditures—to be in the long-range interests of shareholders, employees, and customers as well as the general public.

The supplement went on to illustrate and discuss such concerns as improvements in air and water quality control, management of forests to provide recreational and esthetic enjoyment as well as to meet commercial needs, encouragement of employees to improve their skills and education, hiring and training of members of minority groups, and the reduction of social and racial inequities plus active support of educational institutions.

The Crown Zellerbach Foundation, established in 1952, supports a program of philanthropy exceeding $1,250,000 annually. A special foundation grant of $500,000 helped establish Crown College at the University of California at Santa Cruz. The foundation also provides scholarships and fellowships, including study at West Coast colleges by students and faculty members from southern Negro colleges.

This, then, is the company seeking a steadily growing recognition and a favorable corporate image. The occasion of its hundredth birthday was chosen as a logical and effective means of gaining attention and approval.

Extensive Staff Preparation

An outstanding feature of both the new corporate identity system and the Centennial Year celebration has been the thorough, long-range planning by the company staff. A score of design organizations were interviewed and evaluated before an appointment was made. Estimates of cost and timing for various publications and films were made more than a year or two ahead of target dates. In considering a corporate film and selecting a producer, the company viewed many of the better recent movies and discussed plans with other firms and some producers.

Since introduction of a new symbol and signature and the use of media influencing the image were part of a year-long observation, successive steps in the program were scheduled carefully. The first announcement of the Centennial Year was made in January 1970. A company history in the *Crown Zellerbach Times,* the employee newspaper, also began in March. The annual report was made in March, the major film shown in April, and a revised corporate brochure was scheduled to be published before the end of the year.

In many of the media and company publications marking the Centennial, a separate symbol and slogan were used. The symbol is based on a schematic diagram of the glucose ring, the molecule that makes up the structural framework of cellulose. With its added circles, this is a representation of growth and development. The accompanying legend is: "1870–1970, Foundation for the Future, Crown Zellerbach Centennial."

The commemorative device promptly went into use on letterheads, company booklets, and other graphic materials. It was adapted for desk calendars and other mementos, as an office decoration, on special banners, posters, and program covers for company events, and in newspaper advertising. Since the special symbol was only a reminder of the hundred-year celebration, it was to be phased out in December 1970.

Preparations for the celebration got under way about two years in advance, so that all the materials would be ready and the entire organization enrolled in scheduled activities. One of the first messages from the communications department to management opened with these recommendations:

> The approaching centennial in 1970 presents a rare opportunity to broaden and enhance recognition of Crown Zellerbach's reputation and leadership position among all the company's audiences.
>
> These include customers and prospects, stockholders and the financial community, present and potential employees, community groups in operating areas, local and federal government, and the broad business public.
>
> The Centennial will be stressed in all ongoing communications, including the annual report, the *Crown Zellerbach Times,* speeches and presentations, service award dinners, and the like. A new edition of the corporate brochure and a brief history of the company are also planned. We expect to implement a standard identity program by 1970.

A major feature of the year's program is the corporate motion picture, *Number One Bush*. Again, the communications department proposed to management a film that would look forward to the company's second hundred years, rather than reviewing the past, that would present the corporation's activities of 1970 as a basis for further progress and innovation.

One of the first directives for the proposed film set these objectives.

> To vividly convey Crown Zellerbach's look, spirit, and purpose to these and other audiences during the Centennial Year and beyond, we recommend that the company produce a color motion picture which utilizes the latest in film techniques. . . . In addition to providing an exciting corporate image "centerpiece" for events during the Centennial Year, both inside and outside the company, such a film would be syndicated through regular distribution channels. In this way, it would be seen by a wide audience in North America and abroad over the period 1970–1975.

Special Publications Issued

One of the two major publications for the Centennial Year was a new corporate brochure, replacing one previously issued in 1965. Summing up the purpose of this publication are these directives:

> To answer that most basic question about a corporation—What does Crown Zellerbach do? To portray the company as a diversified manufacturer of paper and paperboard products, and as a more or less significant factor in plastics, building materials, and chemicals.

> [To present] a memorable exposition of the company's major products in use—corrugated containers; flexible packages; molded plastics; building materials; chemicals; newsprint; coated printing papers; multiwall bags; electronic data processing papers; business papers; wrapping papers; disposables.

> [To provide] an explanation of such company characteristics as expansion in related product lines, development of managerial talent from within, planned incremental growth of primary manufacturing facilities, research and development, and of such goals as a steadily increasing return on investment.

Also presented are the company's management and utilization of resources, details of production facilities, distribution, and an impression of the company as a social force, a willing and responsible community citizen.

The illustrated company history, a series of chapters in the *Times*, was assigned to Stuart Nixon, author of the "Redwood Empire" and former publicity director of the Redwood Empire Association. The history makes wide use of illustrations from company files, historical societies, and private collections.

Enforcement of the identity program will be the responsibility of a special task force, with representatives of most company departments in the United States and Canada. The purchasing personnel throughout the organization will be involved, so that paint colors, signs, printed materials, and other identifications will be standardized everywhere.

For the guidance of plant and property managers, outside suppliers, designers, advertising agency people, and everyone concerned with identity or communications, the company is preparing a detailed manual. This will show the standard styles that are to be used and also guard against variations or distortions of the symbol or signature.

Headquarters staff of the corporate communications department is headed by Lowell M. Clucas, with Don Winks as assistant director and Gordon E. Grannis as publications manager. In the field there are two public relations men in Portland, Oregon, and two in Louisiana.

The new corporate film was produced by John J. Hennessy Motion Pictures, an organization that has made other motion pictures for the company. The new identity symbol was designed by Robert Miles Runyan and Associates, and this firm also designed the corporate signature, the 1969 annual report, and the revised company brochure.

Dean Smith, San Francisco designer, created all materials for the Centennial program and organized the system of identification that extends throughout the corporation. Doyle Dane Bernbach is the advertising agency handling the Crown Zellerbach corporate program.

Marcor Convinces the Financial Community

ON July 1, 1968, Montgomery Ward and Container Corporation of America announced a proposed merger to form a new company: The two firms became subsidiaries of the new corporation. It was first assumed in the financial community that the move was primarily defensive, as both companies had been considered targets for acquisition or takeover tenders. Several weeks later, the proposed new company was given the name "Marcor Inc."

This study of Marcor is the case history of a successful public relations program that was almost exclusively directed to the financial community. It was necessarily a crash program, because a new corporation was being announced, based on the merger of two well-known companies, and the consummation of the merger depended on the success of the program. The objectives were relatively simple and the targets were apparent, but the means of gaining attention and conviction had to be worked out quickly and effectively.

There were no immediate problems of educating customers or the general public because the operations, and consequently the identities, of the two partners remained relatively unchanged. The new element, and the one to be presented for acceptance, was the new corporation with a completely new name, a history of only a few days, and an image to be created.

The new Marcor symbol was introduced in the October 1968 interim report.

MARCOR
Montgomery Ward   Container Corporation of America

What was essential was the prompt recognition by security analysts, investors, stockholders, and employees that the amalgamation made sense—that two and two could add to more than four. Although each component was to continue under its existing management and be subject to overall policy direction only, the acceptance of the union was based on the records of the two parts and the possibility that the whole would be greater than the parts.

Announcement Receives Skeptical Response

The idea that Marcor was formed to fight off eager conglomerates was only one reason for skepticism by financial people. In its 98 years, Montgomery Ward had been up and down, and some of its critics did not foresee any recovery from the latest slump. Although management had invested millions of dollars in new stores, expansion, and modernization, the heavy costs involved had restricted earnings, and the price of its stock had not appreciated.

There were 12,500,000 shares of Montgomery Ward outstanding among some 88,000 shareholders—down from 100,000 or more. The stock quotation was down to 22 early in 1968, less than half its ten-year high.

Container Corporation enjoyed a better record of growth and profit, but was considered an unexciting company in a prosaic industry. Discussions had been held with several other firms about merger possibilities, but management had insisted on retaining its identity and control, and no suitable arrangement had been developed.

"Makes no sense," "disquieting and confusing," and "sellout" were among the immediate reactions from analysts and investors to the merger announcement. Few saw merit in the union or the potential for a profitable corporation. It was to this skeptical group that Marcor offered its new identity and image.

The urgent need of financial acceptance was, in part, due to the merger agreement. It was necessary to get approval of stockholders of both corporations and to get Container stockholders to exchange for new securities. Common stockholders of Ward's received one share of Marcor common for each share held, of which 50,000,000 were authorized and 12,586,000 outstanding. Common stockholders of Container were offered a choice of $2 convertible preferred of Marcor, convertible share for share, or $55 face value of subordinated debentures of the new corporation. Marcor would accept no more than 49 percent of Container shares in exchange for debentures.

The unusual nature of the transaction attracted interest, and this was converted to conviction of its merits through the communications program. Equally helpful was the participation of senior executives and their support of the educational campaign, which was carried out by the public relations department of Montgomery Ward and directed by Robert V. Guelich, vice-president. What did he have to work with?

The Former Records

Montgomery Ward is the third largest general merchandise retailer in the United States and the second largest mail-order company. At the end of 1968, it operated 468 department stores, 904 catalog agencies, 695 catalog stores, 10 catalog houses; manufacturing plants for concrete pipe and building materials, 6 paint factories, a life insurance business, and a bank; subsidiaries producing camp trailers, television sets, and other products, a credit company and a real estate firm.

In 1872 Ward launched the first mail-order business and attained leadership in the field. By the 1920s, the company's stock was a market favorite. Yet Montgomery Ward was primarily known for its failure to move into urban retailing after World War II. The regime of Sewell Avery brought an era of extreme conservatism in the post-war period when other businesses were growing and booming. During the war, it will be remembered, he conducted the first one-man sitdown strike in the history of corporate management.

After 1941 no more stores were opened, and Avery, who remained until 1955, left behind him an outdated and creaky mail-order business and a retail organization identified with small towns and rural families. There was almost no penetration of the growing city markets. During the next several years, stores were purchased or opened in the cities, but the business grew faster than the management organization, which was still rural oriented and unsuited to modern mass merchandising.

In 1961 Robert E. Brooker, a former Sears, Roebuck executive, became president and chief executive and, with the help of Edward S. Donnell who later succeeded him as president, started the drive into major markets. He brought into the organization hundreds of experienced merchandisers and managers. But the time was late, and there were problems of suitable locations, insufficient volume in big cities to permit use of the mass advertising media, and need to convert 100,000 employees to modern ideas and methods.

Not all the problems were solved. Some older stores were too small for modern merchandising techniques. Catalog business grew in sales and profits, aided by data processing and improved operation systems, and mechanization of the expanding credit business was nearing completion. Although Chairman Brooker admitted that the rejuvenation of Ward was taking longer than he expected, he pointed to earnings in 1968 that were almost double those of the previous year, earnings per share that were the highest in 15 years. Even more important was the strong momentum toward further growth and profit gains.

Container Corporation was not as large as Ward but has had a more favorable record of growth and earnings. The company was founded in 1926 and is a leading producer of paperboard packaging, well known for packaging ideas and service to producers of consumer goods. Between 1963 and 1967, earnings climbed from $19,125,000 to $32,906,000. The company and its subsidiaries have 128 plants and mills in six nations. The corporation has strong vertical integration, owning or leasing more than 850,000 acres of timberland. Container has been recognized through an unusual series of advertisements, initiated by founder Walter Paepcke, that stressed the great ideas of mankind rather than offerings of merchandise.

It was necessary to convince Wall Street that the combination of these diverse corporations could produce more than just self-protection, that the united organization would have both financial and personnel assets to promote growth and stability. Equally important was a demonstration that Montgomery Ward had turned a major corner, that it was pointed toward growth in areas that would produce higher returns on sales, and that the recent modernization and expansion program of Container Corporation was the start of developments that would increase the firm's share of market and return on invested capital.

The situation was further complicated by possible conflicts between the required disclosure and the restrictions on a firm with securities in registration with the SEC. This left a narrow avenue between stock promotion and full disclosure that was successfully negotiated.

Objectives Were Apparent

There was little opportunity or need for research into the standing of the merging companies, which could be seen from their position in the market. Executives of the two firms were closely aware of their relative positions. The problem was to start a new corporation. Public opinion research could get under way after its inception.

Objectives were equally clear-cut. There was an immediate and urgent need to complete the announced merger by the approval of stockholders and their acceptance of new securities. This required strong support from analysts and brokers, something that could by no means be taken for granted.

Beyond this short-term objective was the longer-range campaign to present Marcor as a successful entity with evident chances for improvement. There had to be a picture of a strongly financed, well-managed, aggressive company with modern ideas and the ability to make them work. Incidental but important target groups were customers and employees, who had questions to be answered, worries to be calmed, and support to be enlisted.

In the first announcement, the autonomy of the two firms was stated jointly by the chief executives.

> These two Chicago-based companies will carry on their separate businesses of manufacturing and retail and catalog selling, under their own names, and will remain in Chicago. We believe that the combined expertise of both companies in their diverse and expanding markets will bring greater benefits to the consuming public in this country and abroad. This partnership will create an organizational environment, offering greater opportunities to our current employees and continuing to attract outstanding personnel.

To win stockholder approval, managements worked together. With the July 1 announcement, special letters were sent to all stockholders from the chief executives. Montgomery Ward also sent a letter from Chairman Brooker to its employees, explaining the preliminary agreement in principle and enclosing all pertinent facts on the amalgamation. One paragraph said,

> It is my firm belief and that of the officers and directors of the company that the combination of the resources of the two companies will enable us to accelerate our growth and expansion plans. This will mean bigger and better opportunities for you and all employees. Our present programs and policies have been producing increased earnings and these are expected to continue to benefit all employees, especially those of us who are members of the Montgomery Ward Employee Profit Savings Plan.

Complete Information Was Supplied

For analysts, bankers, investors, and the financial press, it was decided to provide all possible information on the terms and plans of the proposed merger and on the companies from which it was being created.

This was to be factual information, without interpretation but with full explanation of all details. This campaign had to be started before a name had been announced and prior to corporate meetings of approval.

Unusual activity in Ward stock on July 1, 1968, indicated speculation about the meetings of Ward and Container that had been announced for July 2. As a result, an announcement was rushed out on July 1 about the purpose of the special meetings. At the same time that this announcement appeared on the broad tape, all news media received a release that both boards had agreed to discuss the merger.

After the separate meetings on July 2, in which favorable action was accomplished, special letters were mailed to stockholders. The first press conference was held in Chicago, with senior officers of both firms explaining details of the merger plan and answering the questions of reporters, some of whom were skeptical about the results of this unusual union.

The new corporate child had to have a name and a graphic symbol. Advance work had been done within the design departments of both organizations, principally to insure against any advance leaks. As announced by Chairman Brooker,

> The name Marcor was not decided by a computer, as was the recent textile Qiana, but by the communications and graphic experts. The result is a corporate name that is easy to pronounce, has excellent design potential, and begins with the letter "M" to permit retention of the M symbol on the New York Stock Exchange. Marcor could also be translated into "Marketing Core" or a "Marketing Corps of Management."

Other possibilities considered were M International, Cormont, Montain, and Unicor. It was decided that a primary consideration should be the initial M. In addition to a distinctive Marcor logotype, there is a new corporate symbol to signify that Marcor is a new concept in central management and a structure that can grow in any direction.

Between the first announcement in July and the stockholders' meetings on October 31, a series of news releases flowed to the financial press, analysts, and bankers. An early story confirmed plans for autonomous operation of the companies and that the organization of Marcor would be small and concerned primarily with financing and policy. Officers were named—Robert E. Brooker as chairman, President Leo H. Schoenhofen, president of Container, Gordon R. Worley as financial vice-president, Carl M. Blumenschein, vice-president and controller, Daniel Walker as general counsel, Harry E. Green, president-overseas.

With subsequent releases, the financial community received a series of information sheets with biographies of the key executives, terms of the SEC registration, and digests of the existing position and activities of Ward and Container. This program was helpful, but the financial people were generally unconvinced until it was announced that Container stockholders had agreed to the offer for their stock. This was followed by news of the stockholders' meetings on October 31, affirming the combination and establishing Ward and Container as subsidiaries of Marcor.

President Schoenhofen told stockholders:

> The affiliation will provide desirable diversification and additional financial strength for both businesses. It will provide an opportunity to share the extensive marketing experience of the two companies, while allowing the present management of each to develop its own programs and policies.

A 32-page *Marcor Financial Facts Book* was mailed to more than 20,000 members of the financial community. This was the most important single piece of material. It included ten-year statistical summaries of earnings, sales, dividends, capital, debt, inventories, and net investments, with histories of the two firms and their principal officers.

Acceptance Indicated

Broader acceptance of the new corporation was prompt and was marked by editorial comment. The price of Marcor stock, which opened November 1, 1968, at 44, was up 12 from a year-earlier quotation for Ward. The preferred opened at $46^{1}/_{2}$, compared with Container at $28^{1}/_{2}$ on November 1, 1967.

"Ward Joins the 'Now Generation' " was the title of an extensive article in *Business Week*. "The potential is impressive," reported *The Wall Street Journal*. These and other comments stimulated further programs to make the new corporation known and understood.

Direct contact between executives and analysts had been established at every opportunity, and on November 14, sixty-three New York specialists in retailing companies were flown by charter jet for a meeting with the Investment Analysts of Chicago. The group heard principal Marcor officers, saw 1,500 slides and 60 charts, and toured a new Ward store and a Container plant. Other meetings with analysts and investors were held in Cleveland, San Francisco, Los Angeles, Boston, and Philadelphia.

Full-page advertising appeared in *The Wall Street Journal*, the *New*

York Times, Fortune, Forbes, Time, Newsweek, Barron's Weekly, and other publications. Large, modern-looking illustrations marked the unusual format, and the copy announced and explained the new corporation. It was realized that only a continued campaign would eventually reach all the desired targets, so small-space advertisements appeared regularly in financial papers.

A new note appeared in consumer advertising as well, explained as a bid for a more "swinging" image. Chairman Brooker said, "It will identify with youth. It will also tell customers that they will be surprised, that they will find the unexpected, when they come into one of our stores." Of the new campaign, the advertising agency, E. H. Weiss, said:

> We've tried to give it an unexpected quality; people tend to think of Ward's in a certain way and we've tried to present it differently. People have the feeling that Ward is a stuffy organization, but when they compare different stores they recognize that it's a rather exciting merchandising operation.

Successful completion of the merger and acceptance of the new securities went a long way toward convincing the financial community that Marcor was vitally alive, but as with any firm, it was necessary to show continued results. This was even more critical with Marcor than with other companies, because analysts and investors were looking closely to see if performance equalled promises.

The best evidence would be forthcoming with the year-end statement, but in the meantime interim statements were issued by the two firms that could bolster their position. Montgomery Ward's semiannual report for the six months ending July 31 showed per-share earnings up from 16 cents in the 1967 period to 66 cents. It was pointed out that improved earnings were gained from fewer stores, emphasizing the company's aggressive drive toward larger units in metropolitan centers. Installation of new computer centers for credit business and further revision of catalog merchandising were also reported. Another report sent to analysts and stockholders was the Container statement for the three-month and six-month periods ending June 30, 1968.

As with any corporation with new ventures, investors looked to management as one factor on which to base confidence. When the union was completed, the form and personnel of Marcor management were stated in detail, from which the following statements are taken:

> The role of Marcor executives in the operation of Ward and Container is a blend of outside counselor and parent. While they expect to preserve what is best at each of the companies, they believe Marcor will

introduce a new degree of objectivity, permitting a fresh look at both operations.

Marcor's management expects to remain small and "form free" so that it can respond quickly and effectively to new problems. It plans to draw freely on the management capabilities of both Ward and Container from time to time, assembling task forces to tackle particular projects, and disbanding or reshaping the force as each problem is solved or redefined. . . .

One of the most direct and immediate benefits Marcor is expected to produce is the infusion of many of the specialized management skills and techniques of each company into the other's management force. . . .

Container and Ward have been particularly effective in their programs to develop mature, well-grounded executives and managers because of their decentralized organizations, which give key people a high degree of autonomy of operation while working within broad corporate objectives.

The successful development of these able merchandising staffs has been based on both the recruitment of people with recognized ability and continued training throughout the organization for advancement and responsibility. Ward has presented an incentive to work with recognized retailing leaders and to gain positions that might not be available in the same time at other firms. Generous compensation policies include bonuses, liberal profit sharing, group insurance, and retirement programs. Possibly most important has been the expanded training courses, including some of the most modern and sophisticated management development programs in the industry.

Employees Were All Informed

Although there was no basic change for employees, because both companies continued individual operations, there were questions to be answered and help to be enlisted. The fact that people continued to work for the same company, receive pay checks with the same name, and report through the same organization minimized the need for a new image.

However, Ward has always had a policy of informing employees about its financial situation and corporate developments. Frequent presentations are made through audio-visual media, including motion pictures, film strips, and slides. After the annual report is published, meetings are held with administrative and field employees, using these techniques to interpret the report and the proposed developments. Employees are invited to attend the annual or special meetings or to watch them on closed circuit television.

One of the first steps in the announcement of Marcor was a personal letter to all employees from Chairman Brooker. Bulletins and employee publications kept everyone informed. Ward already had a strong system of communication with its personnel in *Forward,* a monthly paper, distributed to 100,000 employees; *Counter Talk,* a specialized monthly tabloid for catalog sales agencies, and *Management Newsletter,* also a monthly, which covers 3,500 Ward managers and supervisors. Group meetings are regularly held with top corporate and field management, including merchandising department managers and district managers.

Communications to employees are closely linked to the consumer education program, also a function of the PR department. Films promote consumer relations and education in the fields of fashion and grooming, physical fitness, and recreation. This is a steadily growing phase of promotion to consumers. Motion pictures are also used for product publicity, promotion, and other communications. As neither Ward nor Container is identified in consumer advertising as a Marcor subsidiary, there has been no problem of identification with the general public, except when customers want to become investors.

For public relations and customer promotion, Ward is using a series of brief motion pictures. These are made with the assistance of leading sports figures and have a special appeal for young people. They are nationally distributed by film libraries, shown in the company's stores, and provided to luncheons and meetings.

Marcor advertising has been handled by Container's agency, N. W. Ayer, with supervision from the CCA advertising director. Each of the two divisions retains its own advertising agency. Publicity and public relations for Marcor are centered in Ward's organization and are the responsibility of the public relations department under the direction of principal executives of the parent firm. The PR department is headed by a Ward vice-president, who reports to the chairman and chief executive officer. Section managers in various departments recommend programs and budgets, and the PR director presents a composite program to management. Hill & Knowlton has been retained as public relations counsel and Georgesson & Company for proxy solicitation.

Prior to the merger announcement, the physical identification of Marcor, its logotypes and signatures, were developed by the internal staffs of the companies. Earlier, Ward's had researched and redesigned its own corporate logotype to present a more modern appearance. The use of the corporate identity is limited primarily to stockholder communications and reports, corporate letterheads, business cards, displays, and institutional advertising, all of which are primarily concerned with the financial world. There has been no necessity for identity manuals throughout the organization.

In the annual report for 1968, issued April 7, 1969, full advantage of the opportunity to review progress was taken. A joint statement by the chief executives, which opened the report, said:

> This first annual report of Marcor is being sent to approximately 88,000 stockholders, many of whom have been long-time shareholders of Montgomery Ward or Container Corporation. We are pleased to report to these stockholders that results . . . justify their votes of confidence in the merger of their companies into the new corporate growth structure of Marcor. . . . For the full year, earnings increased 43.7 percent to $53.8 million, on sales of $2.5 billion.

The report included separate sections for the developments in each company as well as statements by Marcor executives. Full-color illustrations and modern format were combined to continue the image of a progressive organization.

Results of the campaign, as measured by acceptance by the financial community, are considered more than satisfactory. Marcor securities have been recommended by leading analysts and have been purchased by a growing number of institutions on the basis of full information about the company's problems and prospects. Common-stock prices have been consistently higher than in recent years and have held up well in market dips. Market activity has exceeded the former average combined daily turnover of the two partners.

At mid-1970, Robert Brooker retired as chief executive officer and was named chairman of the executive committee of Montgomery Ward and Container Corporation. Leo H. Schoenhofen became president and chief executive of Marcor. The office of chairman was eliminated.

At the same time, the stock of Marcor was split two for one and the dividend increased from $1.00 to $1.60 per share annually.

Marcor was cited by the Public Relations Society of America for the most outstanding investor relations program of 1968, and in 1969 it received additional citations from *Financial World* magazine for its annual report and published report of its annual stockholder meeting.

Index

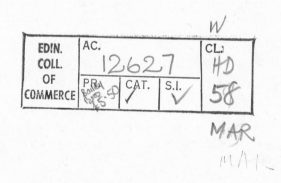